# Get Your Hands Dirty
## Mission in Action

edited by

Doug Priest and Nicole Cesare

Dedicated
to
Walter and Iva Lou Birney

… who are most comfortable when nothing is said about them

# Contents

Preface                                                                    vii

## Let's Go

1.  Wait No Longer                                                          1
    *Carol Plymale*

2.  We Aren't on Acme Tours                                                 7
    *Janice Lemke*

## Let's Listen

3.  The Power of Listening                                                 27
    *Luis Bush*

4.  What Would Jesus Do About Poverty?                                     49
    *Ashley Barker*

5.  Compassion with an Attitude                                           61
    *Bryant L. Myers*

6.  Toward a Missiology of Transformation                                 77
    *Charles Van Engen*

## Let's Work

7.  HIV/AIDS: Avenues of Involvement for the Church                       93
    *Doug Priest*

8.  Changing a Community                                                  101
    *Florence Muindi*

9.  Saved to Serve: Finding Motivation for Ministry                      117
    *Cory and Janice Lemke*

10. Who are the Least of These and How do We Serve Them?                 123
    *Pamela L. Sanders*

11. Sharing the Gospel on Treadmills and Spin Bikes                      137
    *Janet Smith*

12. Building the Kingdom Brick by Brick                                   143
    *Lyndon and Denise Pesho*

Contributors                                                              149

Acknowledgements                                                          150

# Preface

Jesus proclaimed release to the captives, provided sight to
the blind, fed the hungry and became Good News to the poor
(Luke 4:18-19). All across the land, Christians are recovering
a sense of urgency in meeting the needs of those who are
hurting, doing so in the name of Christ.

Churches, small groups, Sunday school classes, students and
preschoolers are looking beyond the church doors to find
opportunities to serve the community, the region, the nation
and the world.

*Get Your Hands Dirty* is a collection of articles, anecdotes,
and case studies that illustrate the ways God's people involve
themselves in His mission to His Creation. From renovating
a run-down school classroom to constructing homes for the
survivors of hurricane Katrina, from starting churches in
Ukraine to providing home care for those dying from AIDS,
God wants His people to get up, get out, and get moving!

It's time. Read on.

# 1

# Wait No Longer

by Carol Plymale

"**Y**ou Haven't Lived Until the Kids Are Out of High School and the Dog Is Dead!" read a headline on the front of the magazine in the checkout lane at the grocery store. All I could do was stare at it. Our youngest son was graduating from high school, our daughter was graduating from college and getting married, and we had recently put our seventeen-year-old dog down because of health problems. I was in mourning for the changes in our lives that were occurring. Was this article directed towards me? I bought that magazine. The article suggested that we who have completed the "hands-on parenting" part of our lives are free now to pursue many opportunities that were not possible before because of family responsibilities.

We were not yet at retirement age but were approaching it. My husband was a manufacturing engineer and I was a nurse. We loved working together doing a lot of different things such as home improvement and building projects. We enjoyed traveling in our motor home. We were active in our church, especially in the missions program, and were team leaders for several short-term mission trips. We had talked about our retirement years, but had not yet developed a vision for them. God had been so good to us. He asked for laborers for the harvest. Was it possible that we could do something in our retirement that used the various skills and interests that God had given us in our lifetime? If so, what would that look like? We hadn't a clue, but we talked and prayed more.

We inventoried our lives and resources. Mission work was our passion. We liked to travel. Virgil could use his engineering and building skills. I could use my organizational and nursing skills. Both of us had some computer knowledge. We owned a motor home. The vision grew. We could sell our home and move full-time into our motor home. This would free us up financially, as well as eliminate the time and resources needed to maintain a house. We would be able to go where the Lord might direct us and have our own housing! We would commit three months each year to helping out on a mission project. We were excited and told our children and church friends of our vision for the future so there would be some accountability for our decision. Later, on a June evening, we motored to the church parking lot for our first night of retirement living in our motor home. This was not the beginning of our journey. The Lord had started this journey many years before by giving us experiences we could use now.

We have often been asked if taking this step was difficult. The answer is both "yes" and "no." We read many books on living full-time in an RV. We attended several seminars on the subject. We talked with people who were full-timing. We had had our motor home for seven years and camping was a family activity all our lives. But that first night in the church parking lot was an interesting one. There was a terrible storm. The sky got black. The wind pushed our motor home around so much that I became frightened. Ohio has tornados, and we no longer had a basement! I cannot deny that the thought, "What have we done?" came into my mind. But the storm did calm, and both the motor home and I stopped shaking.

Then there was the work getting rid of our stuff. We were committed to the new lifestyle so we decided not to put our things in storage. We went through thirty-eight years of pictures and slides as well as household items that we would no longer be able to use because of space. Our walk-in closet items had to be sorted out to fit into seventeen inches of hanging space. Discussions were held. If you are married, you know the kind of discussion I mean. We purchased two notebook computers. Living together in about 100 square foot of space would be trying enough, but sharing a computer would put us over the line! We laughed a lot and also cried a few tears. However, getting rid of things turned out to be an incredibly freeing experience. We were reminded of the story of the rich young ruler and understood better why Jesus asked the young man to give his riches away.

Since we had been on the missions committee for years, we knew that there were many opportunities for service in the US. Armed with a letter of introduction from our minister, our first destination was a mission agency in Indianapolis. We also obtained a ministry directory that lists various mission groups. We joined SOS (Servants of Our Savior), a mission organization for RV'ers. We had attended the National Missionary Convention for years and knew that it would be one of the best places to share our desire to be of assistance. We went again that fall.

Since we retired four years ago, we have participated in a variety of mission projects at various Christian camps, schools, churches, and missions agencies. The work was varied. We painted, washed dishes, repaired items, did electrical, plumbing, and carpentry work, worked on computer tasks, sewed, organized items, and so on. It was the kind of mission work we expected.

But the Lord had something unexpected for us. Our motor home does not travel across the seas, but we did on two occasions.

I was in my last semester of college and about to leave for my last Christian Fellowship retreat as a college student when I got a phone call from God. Okay, so it wasn't really God's voice I heard at that moment, but it was God's call being spoken in my heart. The person on the other end of the phone asked, "So, what do you think about going to Southeast Asia for two years to teach English as a second language?" Needless to say, I asked for some time to mull this one over with God before giving an answer.

Wouldn't you know it, the main speaker at this retreat challenged all the college students to give at least two years of service to God overseas after graduation. God wasn't about to let me off the hook. The last evening of the retreat I went on a hayride with all my friends, the friends I had for years in college, the ones who stood by me through everything. As we were having a great time and the hay fight began, I sat at the back of the trailer and started to pour out my heart to God.

"Why are you calling me to leave all these great friends? Why are you asking me to go so far away? Where exactly is this country? Aren't there tons of kids in the public schools here who need a Christian influence? Why do you want me to go to Asia when I hate rice?" After all the questions came out, I came back to the one that was hardest for me. How could I leave everything and everyone I knew and loved to go to a place I didn't even know that much about?

Through the tears of letting go, I felt the assurance that He would be enough for me, that He is sufficient. There is no one who could ever be more sufficient than Him. That was nine years ago. I have been living in a country in Southeast Asia for the last eight years. There is nowhere I would rather be. The situation of the government and the overall environment in my country right now are perfect to make a huge impact for Christ. The people are confused because all they have been taught and all they have known has collapsed around them. They are open and looking for new answers.

**Janelle, serving in Indonesia**

We went to China for two months to help with a marketplace ministry. My husband Virgil served as the office manager and construction supervisor for a new factory building. Then another call came and we went to Thailand. Virgil was needed to manage the construction of another Business as Mission ministry effort, a fitness and learning center. We stayed on this project almost six months. And we have been so blessed! It is indescribable how fulfilling these experiences have been.

Although I have told you of our journey, what about you? You, too, have been given a past that the Lord wants to use. What is it that you enjoy? The Lord gets pleasure from seeing you enjoy doing His work. Do you like gardening, cooking, bookkeeping, babysitting? God has a place for you. How about teaching, driving, skiing? God has a place for you to put those past experiences to work for His glory. Sometimes the difficult thing to do is to see that you are invaluable to God's plan. You are. No one can do what you have been prepared to do, but you must be willing to commit to sharing your past.

You can start by participating in a short-term mission project. The experience should give you an overview of a mission as well as encouragement from the small group structure. Or you might start by contacting a mission in your area and telling them a bit about your background. They may have a job waiting just for you. Contact a person on your mission committee. It is a pleasure to hear people say they are interested in giving their experiences to missions. They will direct you to opportunities for service.

When you volunteer, you may ask for some considerations. For instance, physical labor may not be something you can do. Let the mission know what you are capable of. You may want to limit to the hours available or the time of the year. Perhaps you will need housing; it may be available. Talk over your needs with the mission and your church family. We are blessed by the prayer support we receive from our family, church family, and friends. And if you are not able to participate in a mission project at this time, consider being a prayer and financial partner for someone close to you.

I have come to believe that the article that struck me so at the grocery store was written in order to move us to do God's will. The person who wrote the article wrote it at the right time and the article was placed right before my eyes. You may not need something so dramatic, but you do need to consider how God wants you to use what no other person on this earth has but you. You are unique. There is something that you can do that no one else in this world can do at a particular time in a particular place when that particular thing is needed. You just have to say to the Lord and others that you are willing to go. He will see that you get to the right place at the right time. Go and find how very blessed you will become. Then write an article and let us all know about your experience. We can't wait!

# 2

# We Aren't on Acme Tours: Keys to Successful Short-Term Ministry

by Janice Lemke

The church Loyall Watkins serves as missions pastor in Graham, Texas, isn't all that big or special. Some 400 to 450 people attend on any given Sunday -- mostly blue-collar workers. Nevertheless, they have big ambitions. "We hope to turn out ministers and missionaries and not just church members," says Loyall. They also want to start 1000 churches in 20 years. He admits that is a huge goal and sees the importance of partnering with others in order to reach it.

Perhaps a generation ago, they'd simply send money for mission work and let someone else do it, but now church members want to be personally involved. Some say sending teams is too expensive and wonder if they really accomplish anything of value. Loyall believes, however, that personal involvement in missions has resulted in both fruit on the field and spiritual growth for those who participate.

Loyall heard about our mission work in Ukraine and emailed us, hoping we could link him with a worthwhile project. My husband, Cory, along with several local church leaders, had started a training program designed to equip men to evangelize and plant churches. They added seminars on evangelism, wanting to mobilize all believers rather than a few "professionals." We had served in Ukraine a little over six years when we got his letter, and we shared a similar goal of seeing many churches started in Ukraine. Nevertheless, we felt hesitant to invite him, still recovering from the stress of another short-term team. The leader of that group refused to take advice and brought more harm than good to the cause of Christ and to the reputation of the local church. Loyall seemed to have a different attitude, however: humble and willing to serve.

He wrote to us, "It is our desire to be a blessing to our missionaries and the people to whom we minister. I understand that you know your field and we don't. I'll take any advice you want to give. I believe God has blessed me with good insight into missions ministry and cultural matters, but I am still learning and growing and want to remain teachable."

We decided to match Loyall and his team with Victor Olenik, a pastor/evangelist. Victor had once belonged to the local mafia, but came to Christ through his wife, grew in his faith, and shared it with others. He joined our first church planters' training course and started groups in six villages. Wanting to multiply his efforts, he discipled young men who accepted Christ and took them along when evangelizing or leading groups.

Victor agreed to host the team of six from Texas, but his wife had a few apprehensions. Cory dropped me off at their house on his way to meet the team. I found Olya outside their home, feeding ducks and chickens and collecting water. "The water is on for only two hours in the morning and two in the evening," she said, dumping another bucket into a bathtub under a fruit tree nearby. She hurried to the summer kitchen, a shed behind their house, stirred a pot on the small gas stove, and accepted my offer to help make lunch. While peeling potatoes for borscht, I learned she would be feeding the group all their meals throughout the week. "I'm not afraid of the work," she said, "but I'm praying they will stay healthy. American stomachs don't always adapt very well to a different diet."

She also wondered how they'd respond to using an outhouse – the Ukrainian version is a small, wooden shed with a hole in the cement floor. Victor wanted to have the Americans stay in better housing, with church members who have apartments and indoor toilets, but they were too embarrassed to have foreigners stay in their shabby dwellings, so he decided to keep the team. Olya is very hospitable, but she had heard about an American team who stayed in a village and made a big deal among themselves after one member used the outhouse. The host did not understand the words, but understood the meaning very well. I tried to assure her that this group had been to Ukraine before and they would be fine. I hoped my words would be true.

By the end of the week, Olya said, "It will be hard to see them go. They've become like family." Victor was equally thrilled by the genuine contribution they'd made to the ministry.

# Strategic

In order to reach the goal of 1000 churches in 20 years, Loyall realizes the need to act strategically. When taking teams to Ukraine, or any other country, he wants to do more than simply give Americans an interesting cultural experience. "With every short-term trip, we are working toward a long-term goal," he says. "I've seen village after village in Ukraine that needs a church."

In Crimea alone -- a peninsula extending into the Black Sea -- over 1000 villages have no church. These villages are filled with people who do not know Christ. With the need so great, where could he start? He knew he needed to partner with someone already in place with a similar ambition, someone who could make good use of the team's energy and resources. "When we go and work with Victor," he says, "we work toward the goal of seeing more churches started in Ukraine."

Victor has also learned to think strategically. Along with other Ukrainian pastors and evangelists who have caught the vision, he is working toward the goal of a church for every town and village of Crimea. When choosing where to start a church, he focuses on nearby villages where people are receptive; for example, where at least one Christian already lives who wants neighbors to come to Christ. He plans an evangelistic event, perhaps shows the *Jesus* film, and continues to hold meetings where people respond. He seeks to develop congregations with a similar evangelistic outlook. He gives extra attention to discipling men who come to Christ and trains them as leaders.

In his own village, people didn't respond for a long time -- they did not trust him, knowing he had been in the mafia. They watched his life for ten years before they acknowledged he was a changed man. When he showed the *Jesus* film again, they were ready. A growing church now meets in his hometown. With help from the men he is training, Victor has started groups in ten villages. The Americans come and go, but Victor and his helpers provide follow-up on contacts they have made.

# Advance Preparation

Loyall likes to form teams no less than six months in advance, to give team members time to raise funds and arrange for time off work. They need to obtain passports, gather supplies, and make travel arrangements. Practical details aside, they also need to get in the right frame of mind. The group meets regularly to plan and to pray for their ministry and for the on-going work in Ukraine.

To emphasize his expectations, Loyall requires each participant to sign a statement agreeing to certain behaviors and attitudes, such as servanthood, Christ-like behavior and respect for the host's view of Christianity and approach to ministry. "They need to recognize that we are going as guests," says Loyall, "and that we will work under the authority of the local pastor. The local church is there for the long term, and they understand their culture better than we do. We don't go there to tell people, 'This is how we do it in America.'" He expects team members to refrain from complaining, gossip, romantic involvement, and negative comments about the country's politics. Meanwhile, the host needs time to prepare, too. When we visited Victor and Olya in the spring, they showed us the huge garden they had planted and the baby chicks which would help feed the team that fall. Before the group arrives, he obtains literature, contacts village authorities for meeting permits, rallies church members to pray and recruits people to help cook or evangelize. We help find interpreters, arrange for transportation, and act as a communication go-between.

Contacts Victor makes while taking care of logistics sometimes bear fruit. I talked with a woman at his church who said she met Victor when he brought the Americans' passports to the police station where she works. She felt nervous about attending the meetings, but people were friendly, the music was good and the preaching touched her heart. Two months later, she gave her life to Christ. "I regret only that I didn't come to Christ sooner," she said. "I wasted so many years. I've been married five times. I've had so many abortions, I can't even count them. I still have problems, but God helps me each day. Before, I didn't even want to live." She expected her co-workers at the police station to respond negatively when they learned she had joined the evangelical church, but she was pleasantly surprised. She reads a devotional booklet to them and they listen. As she talked, I thought of the Samaritan woman, who after her brief encounter with Jesus became an effective evangelist in her village.

# Plan for Ministry

We have used teams in various ways in Ukraine: to help with Vacation Bible School, medical work, and music ministry. The group from Texas initially came to help with evangelism, going door-to-door in villages; with their third visit, they added a medical component. We have not met many Americans this eager to talk to others about their faith, but for many team members, it was not their first experience with evangelism.

Loyall told me, "We teach Christians how to share the Gospel themselves, not just invite people to church for the pastor to explain the way to salvation. We believe in the priesthood of all believers." Not all team members felt confident, however, so he helped them prepare for ministry in Ukraine. He asked each person to write out his or her testimony, and he coached them on how to lead others to Christ. They paired up and practiced telling the story using the Evangicube, a picture cube illustrating the basic Gospel message.

During their first trip, Victor arranged for them to visit six villages -- ranging in size from 500 people to around 3000 -- where he had started churches. Team members split up and went door-to-door with an interpreter and a local evangelist. "In all these villages, people are open to the Gospel," he told the group, "and they are expecting your visit." Besides sharing their faith, they invited people to a meeting that evening.

"How did it go?" I asked the team when I visited them at the end of the week. Sometimes they went to the homes of people that Victor knew. Sometimes they just initiated conversations at the market or as they walked down the street. Some people yelled at them or did not want to listen, but overall, they found many who were open to hearing about the hope Jesus offers.

In the wake of Hurricane Katrina, we were working in a neighborhood in Metairie, LA. Looking down the street in either direction, we saw people too overwhelmed to make any headway restoring their homes. Our team was tearing out flooring and ripping out drywall so effectively that we decided to talk to some neighbors to see where we could help more.

Barbara was sitting on the back of her car at the entrance of her driveway. When we asked how the work on their house was going, she said she was sick and weak and couldn't stand to go into the house anymore. Her son and cousin were inside. We asked whether she wanted help from ten more workers. Barbara looked flush and said, "You've been sent to me by the Lord."

"So, that's a yes?"

A new van of Georgia Tech volunteers arrived, and I accompanied them to Barbara's house. She told us to go on in where her boys were already working. I found both of them in the main room and said, "Barbara sent us in here to help. Is there anything we can start doing?" The cousin looked at us from behind his surgical mask – we were wearing the masks in addition to hazmat suits. He made eye contact, looked over to the son, looked down. Then, he turned to walk back into a dark room, leaving us alone in silence. There was standing water in the den, mold everywhere you looked. We stood in strange silence as the son disappeared into another dark area. We followed the cousin.

I introduced myself again. "We're here to help; we'll do anything. Just let us know where to start."

To this attempt, the cousin slowly looked at us and said, "Don't open that." He nodded his head toward a decrepit refrigerator.

Through our work in hurricane recovery after Katrina, we had come to learn that the refrigerator is the center of all disgust that the wreckage had rendered into a home. We understood.

The cousin began to pick up debris as though we were no longer there, so we attempted once again to make a connection. "This is Tayo. He will be in charge of our volunteers, so let him know what needs to be done. And if you need anything else, he can let us know." With that, I encouraged a couple of our leaders and left to check on other teams and restock our water.

We returned an hour later to Barbara's home. Susan and I talked to her on the way in. She seemed to have energy that we saw nothing of during our first visit. She smiled and stopped us to tell stories. After hearing about her famous soul food restaurant, we continued inside to check on the progress.

We entered the front door to find the cousin sweeping and smiling in an emptied out room. The change in the house was dramatic, only an hour later. Our workers were moving quickly and cheerily, taking care of business. The house had thick mold everywhere. There was standing water in the den. Cabinets were destroyed – or needed to be. Furniture was strewn around and debris was everywhere. The entire house was covered with noxious mold, so the floors were slick and the walls were dark.

I asked the cousin how work was coming along. "These workers are amazing. They have cleaned out the whole house. It's going great." He was smiling with his mask off. I asked where the son had gone. "Oh, he's out getting drinks for everybody. It's so hot in here, but he'll be back really soon."

We were completely taken aback by the change in the cousin. The son had not even looked at us before. They had seemed like walking dead, and they seemed to resent us for being there. After those ten guys and girls completely  gutted the house, the visible change was remarkable. But what was more incredible was the change we saw in Barbara and her two boys after only one hour. That team of workers took on difficult circumstances in a dark, moldy house. Giving themselves in those circumstances brought back hope and life to people who expected no one to help them. The house looked amazingly better, but Barbara's family was made brand new.

Before we left later that day, Barbara and her boys overwhelmed us with love. They insisted we take gifts of baseball caps that her son sold. They invited us back for soul food. They showed us how much they had changed because some college students worked hard and got very dirty.

**Rob, preparing for service**

One American said she would call out to someone, "Hello," and her translator would interpret. If the person stopped, she would continue, "I've come here from America in order to share my faith." She told of one woman who invited her home and cried while hearing her message. The woman prayed and gave her life to Christ.

Another told about a negative experience that turned around. A middle-aged woman shouted at her, "Why do you bother to come here? You don't understand how hard life is in Ukraine. God has abandoned us." She decided that conversation would not be fruitful and started down the dirt road. Then an old woman working in the garden, the mother of the first, began yelling at her too. The American felt tempted to "shake the dust off her feet" and move on, but stopped and asked, "Why are you mad at me?" The barrier came down and the older woman listened with tears about God's love and prayed, asking God for a fresh start in life.

A man told of a woman in her mid-40s who said she felt empty inside and had no reason to live. He explained how God can fill that empty place, and she determined to follow Christ. The local evangelist who accompanied him said he had worked with this woman for a year already, but it finally clicked with her.

The Texas team began taking doctors and nurses to Ukraine after learning that medical help would draw people to the church and meet a genuine need. Professional health care is scarce or non-existent in most villages. Our teammate, June Johnson, a registered nurse, serves with a church-based clinic in Ukraine and helped facilitate their outreach. Part of the team went door-to-door, as in previous visits, while the medical personnel saw patients. Some spent time with people waiting for medical care. Each day, they worked in a different village, and each night they held a meeting in that village.

Dr. Howard Johnson wrote later about the experience: "Without the use of modern diagnostic equipment and tests, I felt medically powerless, as all we could do was use simple tools and give out limited medication from our very basic pharmacy. June, however, corrected me by reminding me that our real purpose was introducing people to the love of Jesus Christ. It would have been very frustrating for the medical team except for the incredibly grateful patients who kiss and hug you for just listening to their story."

The medical outreach opens doors for Victor long after the team leaves. Those who came to see a doctor filled out a form, providing names and addresses. The first medical team gave Victor the addresses of over 400 people, and the next year, over 600. These contacts keep him busy all year. When visiting these people, he asks, "Is there something you'd like me to pray for you about?" And a few weeks later, he returns to see how God moved. Even though God often answers his prayers, it does not mean that all are ready to follow Christ. Victor, then, simply asks for more prayer requests.

## Gracious Guests

Unlike the group of Americans Olya heard about, the Texas team managed to use the outhouse without gasping for air afterward. Or if they did, she did not notice. Loyall tried to prepare them for differences they would face in Ukraine. He asked us for guidelines for proper dress and behavior. The women packed skirts and dresses instead of pants, and married women took head scarves to wear during church services. He encouraged them to eat, at least a little, of the food served. He told the group, "I don't want to see anyone making faces. We are getting the best they have to offer."

Americans can sometimes be loud and rowdy, so he advised team members to keep a low profile while traveling and living in Ukraine. Americans are also comparatively wealthy, but careless giving can create problems. Loyall told the group,

"Don't flash money around and don't promise the moon. If someone comes to you with a financial need, see me, and I will talk to Victor."

He challenged them to look for ways to help their host. "There's a lot of work to be done," he said. "You'll see Sergei (Victor and Olya's son) running back and forth carrying water. Grab that bucket of water. Look for ways to chip in and help with chores. We are not staying in a hotel. They are not our slaves."

Americans were not the only ones to adapt; Victor and Olya tried to make things nice for their guests, knowing they came from a different culture. They wallpapered the outhouse and added a can of air-freshener. Although they usually eat meat just once a week, they served meat to their guests at almost every meal. Olya worked from early morning until late at night, cooking for and serving the team.

# Flexibility

I asked Loyall what his group does if things do not go as expected. "They never do," he replied. "Our motto is: 'Be flexible.' I tell groups, 'We aren't on Acme Tours. We want to make an impact in villages.'" People in rural areas often follow the sun more than the clock.

A group may need to adjust more than their daily schedule, since unexpected events can change the ministry focus. During the Texas team's second visit to Ukraine, Victor's right-hand helper died in a car accident soon after their arrival. The church had met in her house when it began in that village. She served the church in many ways and helped Victor with outreach. The team had planned to hold a big evangelistic meeting there, but Victor told them that would show a lack of respect for the dead. They followed his counsel and worked in other villages instead.

Nevertheless, God turned the tragedy into an evangelistic opportunity. The woman was a teacher and school was canceled for her funeral. Over 400 people attended. In Ukraine, Christians use funerals as an opportunity to explain why they have hope, and how listeners can too. One of the interpreters wrote us, "I know that we could not gather all those people for revival meeting, but God used Lilya's departure from this life to open up the Truth for people. Can you imagine 400 people, 90% of them nonbelievers, heard about God's plan for them! Heaven became so very real for us as believers and for nonbelievers even more! Praise the Lord."

At the funeral, Lilya's son, Alexi, realized he was not right with God, and if he were to die as unexpectedly as his mother, he would never see her again. He gave his life to Christ and later decided to quit his job as a manager on a large farm. The job did not give him time for anything but work, and it required that he cheat people and lie. He told me, "I knew I couldn't live that way. And there are not enough people serving God. My mother helped with evangelism, and I need to take her place." Victor began training him to lead groups and share his faith. When the Texas team returned, Victor encouraged Alexi to go door-to- door with them. "I went, even though I didn't understand the Bible very deeply," he said. "But I understood it was God's will. A disciple doesn't just sit."

# Long-term commitment

Ever since the Texas church began working with Victor, they have returned every year; as of this writing, they have come six times. This strategy has several advantages. Team members can build on relationships begun in previous trips. People remember them, and it adds to their credibility. Team members can also see fruit from previous visits.

Loyall leads teams to several countries each year, but he told me, "When people go to Ukraine on an outreach, I want them to get hooked into relationships in Ukraine. I don't want them to try to go to Uganda the next year. We're not in this to give Christian tours to exotic places. We want to invest in relationships for the long-term."

During her second visit to Ukraine, Linda Pippin recognized a man in church she had witnessed to the previous year. She had been waiting for another team member when this man walked by, looking shabby and depressed. As she told him how he could have forgiveness of sins and a relationship with God through Jesus, tears came to his eyes. "You could tell it really clicked with him," she said.

While Linda was sharing the Gospel with someone during her third visit, a woman came up and said, "What these people say is true. My husband and I talked to them two years ago and gave our lives to Christ. My husband used to drink and beat me. He is a changed man. I am different too." Linda asked her later if they had been thinking about Christianity before that conversation. "No, we decided to follow Jesus right then."

Not all contacts turn out that well. Loyall recalled his conversations with the husband of Lilya, the woman who died. After the funeral the husband said, "My wife has been the spiritual strength of the family and now it's time for me to step up." When Loyall saw him the next year, he looked depressed and said life was hard. A couple months later, he hanged himself.

Their son, Alexi, on the other hand, has continued to grow as a Christian and joined our leadership training program. Going door-to-door with the Texas team also strengthened his faith. He told me, "I was amazed to see how the Spirit of God worked in people who weren't interested in the Gospel, but became open to hearing about Jesus and His love. A couple times, I was certain we would be tossed out the door, but I asked them to give us three minutes to share the story of Christ, and then we would go quietly. Some listened not just three minutes, but by the hour. Some of them repented, and after they prayed, they said that God had lightened the load on their hearts."

"It all adds up to make it more than a cultural experience," Loyall said. "These are real people on the other end of the line. I know them, and I love them."

Likewise, we have seen Victor's long-term commitment. His daughter lives in the U.S. and wants him to move there. He has other priorities. After visiting her, he said, "It's nice to have hot water whenever you want it, but there's more to life than hot water." He summed up why he continues in ministry by saying, "I hurt for the world. They are dying without Christ. God loves them and wants them to know Him."

# Humility

Life includes learning experiences; mission work does too. Loyall admitted after the most recent trip, "I made some major mistakes." For one thing, he understood Victor's attitude had been "The more the merrier," so he planned big. Cory told him that twelve people puts too much stress on local resources, but by then, it was too late. Loyall promised to limit group size in the future.

Loyall had asked every team member to be prepared to share a testimony. He told us later, "I should have listened to the testimonies ahead of time. I didn't realize how many on the team had been divorced. The divorce was so traumatic that they included it in their testimony." Just one person spoke about it before Victor objected. Loyall encouraged the others to focus on other aspects of how God worked in their lives.

A weaker leader might have bristled if told, "I don't want to hear any more about divorce" -- after all, divorce is a big problem in Ukraine too. Nevertheless, the local church believes that divorce, especially divorce as a Christian, disqualifies you for leadership in ministry. Loyall simply acted on his campaign

"So you have a mechanical engineering degree, worked at Procter & Gamble, and now you're doing what?"

"Campus ministry in Mexico City."

"How did you end up there?"

I get questions like this all the time. My uncle asked me when I was coming back home to get a "real job." A real job means that you work in the field that you got your degree in. That is the most logical path, isn't it? One thing I have had the pleasure of learning is that, in following Christ, the most logical path is not necessarily God's path. God knows what is best for us, what fits, what is most fulfilling, and where we can be most useful. He is the only one who really knows that for each of us.

I received my bachelor's degree in mechanical engineering from Georgia Tech in 1997, and worked at a co-op at Saturn in Springhill, TN, as a process engineer, design engineer, and project engineer. After graduation, I moved to Cincinnati to work for Procter &

Gamble in project management. I loved motivating others to do their work well and on time, as well as managing all of the aspects of each new project.

After working at P&G for about a year, I was presented with an opportunity to be part of an international campus ministry to college students in Mexico City. My initial reaction: "This really isn't the right time." I was happy with my job, my friends, and my church. But God kept tugging at my heart, and I eventually decided to be a part of this team.

Looking back, it amazes me how God prepared me for exactly what I do now, something that I never would have imagined doing. My Spanish ability, experiences as a leader, and involvement in sport teams have all played a part. Also, my engineering training and

experience prepared me for what I do today. As the Mexico City campus ministry team leader, I ensure that we set strategy and evaluate, make sure the team works together well, motivate team members and interns to do good work and grow, run meetings, keep things organized, manage the work, and communicate with our US steering committee. I have even had the opportunity to use my negotiating skills as we look for a building for our future campus house. I am also responsible for a leadership group of students and for our interns, teaching them and helping them to grow spiritually. In many ways, I am still a project manager.

In Mexico City, I have grown in the ability to lead, manage, and motivate at a much faster rate than I would have in any other job. I have been stretched and have learned so much about myself because I care about what we are doing. I care whether a student finds Christ or not. I care that our team gets along and works well together. I have learned and grown in the gifts God has given me, as well as in areas that were not natural talents. I have confronted difficult situations that I would have left at work before. I am absolutely where God wants me to be. He orchestrated all of my preparation that allows me to be effective in ministry.

God's plans are an adventure. He will prepare us in His way. He has something unique for each of us, and sometimes we get trapped by what we are "supposed" to do. We should be free to follow Christ to the place that He has prepared especially for us.

**Pam, serving in Mexico**

policy: "Respect the knowledge, insights and instructions of the church or person with whom we are working. Our team is there for a short while, but the local church is there for the long term."

Loyall likes to get feedback before returning to the U.S., or soon afterward, and asks, "Is there something we could do better next time?" This attitude of teachability and servanthood makes it easy to welcome his team back.

# Partnership

When Jesus sent out His disciples for ministry, He told them to look for a "man of peace." If a team is going to a region lacking Christians, finding and cooperating with receptive people will advance the mission. Where a church already exists, it is more effective to serve alongside local believers with a similar vision, than simply present an American program. Victor was that man of peace for the Texas team; their cooperative effort met complementary goals.

Victor acknowledges the value of having teams come, since many people like to talk to "exotic" Americans. On the other hand, Loyall says, "We can't think that things are happening just because of us. Victor and others are out there, working hard the whole time we are absent."

Perhaps the value of partnership is best summed up by a Ukrainian evangelist who said, "It's not that they are better or we are better; both sides have something to contribute."
When people come to Christ, who can claim credit? Victor faithfully lives the Christian life in his village and provides follow-up. The Americans generate interest. One plants, another waters, but God causes the increase.

let's
listen

# 3

# The Power of Listening

## by Luis Bush

An emerging Christian leader recently emailed me with words that still ring joyously in my ears. He wrote, "Thanks for being a listening ear. God is moving in my mind and heart— clarity is beginning to emerge." Even if you do not say anything, there is power in listening. How many times have I come away from a meeting with someone and thought as the writer of Proverbs observed, "I did not listen" (Proverbs 5:13). How many times has someone walked away from a conversation with me and thought that very same thing? When we do all the talking, we limit the power and provision of listening.

The theme of the annual gathering of the American Society of Missiology in 2004 was collaboration. Its sub-theme posed the question: Might collaboration be the missing link in Christian world mission? The program for the event alerted us to the fact that "serious examples of collaboration between the more traditional Western church and the rapidly growing expressions of church on mission in the Southern Hemisphere are few and far between" (American Society of Missiology 2004). The need for effective listening increases with the demographics of the Majority World church shifting south and east with its diverse expressions of church. The call has gone out. "It is time to listen to voices from the non-Western world that can help construct a theology capable of empowering the global church for participation in the missio Dei" (Shenk 2001:98).

Listening, after all, is hard work: "Research shows that when a person truly listens, the heart beats faster, more blood circulates, and body temperature rises slightly" (Smith 1992:343). Most people think about four times faster than most people can talk.

After considering the concept of the power of listening, I will describe my personal journey of the listening mode. I will then reflect briefly on biblical and historical precedent, the purpose in listening, people to be listened to, and finally, an emerging paradigm of mission. My basic thesis is that for anyone concerned about the mission of God, the power of listening is that it unveils the ways and means of God's working on earth.

# Power of Listening

Listening can empower human dialogue. Some in the business community recognize the power of listening and have developed presentations and seminars built upon that theme. For example, demand for effective listening in the marketplace has resulted in two thousand presentations on the topic by Tony Alessandra, who combines business success with extensive academic training. Allesandra describes the disempowering nature of poor listening, which leads to misunderstandings, mistakes, lower employee productivity and morale, missed sales, lost customers, billions of dollars of increased costs and lost profits, and increased employee turnover. His phrase "power listening" describes the way to listen. Active listening: 1) improves the environment at work, at home, and in sales; 2) reduces relationship tensions and hostilities; 3) saves time by reducing mistakes and misunderstandings; 4) reduces employee turnover; 5) leads to early problem solving; and 6) increases sales and profits (Alessandra 1995).

Alessandra has recognized the power of listening in conflict resolution. Not only does it provide an effective means to help identify potential problems and their causes, but it also identifies the ways to resolve issues and to diffuse and work through problems to satisfactory resolutions. Intentionally cultivating the practical skill set he recommends has been necessary and helpful in my own journey.

Jacob Loewen teaches us the power of listening in our own context of mission. His experience reminds us that to be good missiologists, we need to be good listeners. Loewen worked among the Waunana people in Colombia. He became convicted about his judgmental attitude of the Waunana. As his attitude changed from superiority to equality, he became more and more vulnerable, which led to greater openness in relating to the Waunana people. He recognized the importance of speaking and working in the vernacular of the people. In the 1980's he and his wife went to India and spent more and more time listening. He writes, "One of the first qualities that a missionary needs to know is the continuing willingness to learn. This quest is motivated by a genuine concern for and a deep appreciation of a way of life that is different from one's own" (Loewen 2000:30). Listening carefully turned out to be a powerful path toward understanding.

# Personal Journey

Almost three years ago I began a journey in the listening mode. It was born out of a simple desire to hear what God was saying to his people. An e-mail in August of 2000 from Paul McKaughan, president of the Evangelical Fellowship of Mission Agencies, prompted me to embark on this quest. He wrote:

I don't know of any time in my 35 years of mission experience that I have seen or felt mission executives more ready and willing to change and adapt. At the same time, I also don't

Was it possible that a swarming outdoor vegetable market like the one in Arusha wouldn't have jalapeños? I had pushed through the maze of crowded pathways there, finding habañeros, chilis, red, yellow, and green bell peppers, but not a single jalapeño. Of course I didn't really need jalapeños, but my Mexican food withdrawal symptoms were growing with each passing week. I'd narrowed the list of missing ingredients to cilantro and jalapeños. I was determined. I had seen a hopeful young boy clutching bouquets of cilantro, so I knew that was doable. All I had to do now was find that kid after I'd located the jalapeños. Dozens of market ladies called out to me as I looked over their selection. Some sold only onions, others carrots and cucumbers, some proffered only potatoes. A cluster of ladies seemed especially curious at my quest. "What is it that you want?" they asked in grammatically impeccable Swahili.

"Ninahitaji jalapeños — pili pili mkali — na cilantro," I answered in my special confluence of Swahili and Spanish. That brought a lot of laughter and a swarm of vendors with every kind of pepper grown in East Africa. Unfortunately, there were no jalapeños among them. As for cilantro, they were clueless. When I turned away all samples, one seller with a genuine smile asked me to bring them and show her when I satisfied my quest. I agreed.

But with another 20 minutes of jostling through the marketplace, my desire for Mexican food was waning. Everywhere I turned more vendors had heard of my pepper pursuance and offered their best. No jalapeños. Defeated, I retreated to the solace of my vehicle only to see the winning grin of the cilantro kid. It took 11 cents to buy a bunch to fulfill my promise to the woman who would become my friend.

That was how I met Mama Esther. She sells only tomatoes, ginger, and tiny pods of garlic. If she were to sell out her entire stock on any given day she'd gross less than $5. Yet there she stays at least 11 hours a day, 6 days a week, rain or shine.

Since that day whenever I go to the market, I never fail to seek out Mama Esther. I buy a few tomatoes, whether I need them or not. She always looks through her supply to find the very best ones for me, then adds one or two as a special discount for her friend. I slip a few extra shillings into her hand in payment. I ask about her daughter and she inquires about my daughter Rachel. We talk about the weather and God's blessings. One day I took a tube of hand cream to her; on my next visit she had a gift-wrapped packet waiting for me. She presented me with a tiny beaded necklace, bracelet, and earrings -- a gift I treasure for the growing friendship that it represents. I cherish her patience with my Swahili, even when it is laced with Spanish.

**Marty, serving in Tanzania**

know of any period in my career that there is less certainty about what changes to make.

The future is uncertain. We know it will be greatly different but are not sure in which ways it will be different. We know that the patterns of the past are showing "wear" and are in need of repair. In many ways the fit between our strategies and way of thinking does not fit our present reality well. We know that they probably won't move us into the future God has for us. Yet the new paradigms that help us interpret and organize our strategies for the future have not become clear. We seem to be in a time of parenthesis between what God blessed in the past and what He has not yet made clear for the future (McKaughan 2000).

Then I reviewed the survey of church and mission leaders conducted in different North American cities in the late 1990s which saw change coming fast. The survey concludes, "The winds of change are swirling with great intensity around the Christian missionary enterprise. The world is changing radically—economically, politically and religiously" (McKaughan 1989:1). What impacted me most was their comment: "The church in America just will not listen to the church around the world." It was like a clarion call. We need to hear those voices and leaders who are now emerging onto their national, regional, and international scenes, especially in Africa, Asia, and Latin America.

My interest in taking the journey of the listening mode was further enhanced during the final months of the year 2000. An abiding question in my own mind was: Where do we go from here in world evangelization? And so began a quest to know the mind of God through the burdens, visions, and dreams of His people as we move into the future. We compressed the reflective process into a practical instrument, which we called the World Inquiry.

The World Inquiry, short for Evangelizing our World Inquiry, started out as an exercise to probe the minds and hearts of evangelical leaders in the major cities of the world. The World Inquiry began and has continued not as a rigorous, methodologically driven research project, but rather as a listening venture that seeks to tune in to God's voice through His People—especially those voices and leaders who are now emerging onto their local, regional, and national scenes in the Two-Thirds World. I was reminded of the words of John Stott: "Life is a pilgrimage of learning, a voyage of discovery, in which our mistaken views are corrected, our distorted notions adjusted, our shallow opinions deepened, and some of our vast ignorances diminished" (Stott 2001:10).

As we listened to one another and sought God through His Word to hear what the Spirit was saying to the church, we saw streams of church and mission emerging on the periphery of mainline ecclesiastical and mission structures; we shared the visions on the hearts of God's servants and we heard from respected missiologists as to what fresh missiological paradigms are emerging.

# Precedent

There are numerous precedents to intentional efforts to listen that demonstrate the inherent power of the listening process. These often take the form of inquiries. The Bible records an occasion when God mandated an inquiry among the nations: "Thus says the Lord: Ask among the nations" (Jeremiah 18:13). Habakkuk inquired of God, asking Him eighteen questions. David inquired of God and learned the power of listening. On one occasion upon inquiring of God, the response came immediately: "When you hear the sound of marching in the tops of the balsam trees, then be on the alert" (2 Samuel 5:24). David listened to God and consequently was empowered to fulfill this God-given mandate for his time.

I'm a missionary kid. I have lived in Kenya my whole life, and my parents work with the Maasai tribe. I've grown up seeing the amazing things that God has done through my parents, but recently I learned that He can do things through me as well.

Not long ago, I went on a mission trip with my mom to Afghanistan. Although I've always been in missions, I learned on this trip what it means to really serve God. When my family was invited to visit Afghanistan I was excited. When we got there, it was a depressing sight. Pieces of airplanes littered the runway and homeless people lined the streets. Buildings were only shells, bombed out during the war, and soldiers walked through the streets to keep the peace.

When my mother was invited back to Afghanistan a second time, I went with her. We went with a team of 12 people from Kentucky. We had a mobile clinic at the Ministry of Women's Affairs and visited the clinic at Istalif, a rural village outside of the capital. When we had a clinic at Istalif on the first trip it was one of the saddest places I've ever seen. Istalif used to be one of the most beautiful places in Afghanistan before the Taliban came. It had the main orchards and vineyards. It was a large, prosperous village with many trees and a beautiful view. Then, the Taliban came with their "scorched earth" policy and burned every fruit-bearing tree and plant. When we visited before, we had the clinic in a bombed-out hotel building. The village houses were rubble, the trees were scarce. To see Istalif again is one of the most amazing sights. There is a very nice clinic, the houses are built up again, and there are trees and plants once more. It is so beautiful. Istalif, and even Afghanistan, is being rebuilt. After so much war, it's full of so much hope. This hope has been brought by people who care -- by missionaries.

My mother is a doctor, so she saw patients and also helped with midwife training lessons. It was my mother who came up with a project for me on the mission trip. One of my talents is art, and my mother thought I could do art therapy with the children at the clinics. So, while everyone else was busy training midwives, pulling teeth, and seeing patients, I distributed crayons and paper to the children and drew with them.

Art therapy is meant to help the children express what they have been through while having fun. I had thought of some topics for the kids to draw, but I did not have a translator, so the children drew whatever they wanted. Some of the children drew serious pictures. Some drew tanks, military buildings, men without arms and even what looked like a grave. It was obvious that these children have experienced a lot of pain. I only hope that drawing helped them release some of this pain and start healing.

On a trip to Istalif, Sheeba, the daughter of one of the Afghan nurses, came with us. She is 15 and speaks English well. I enjoyed getting to know her and hanging out with her that day. It was such an experience to talk with an Afghan my age. She was smart and laughed all the time.

I taught her tic-tac-toe, and she beat me. I was surprised to discover she likes Indian movies. A girl who has lived in Afghanistan her whole life, and we have seen the same movie. It struck me that we are so similar, yet we have lived in different places our whole lives. I made a friend that day.

When the plane landed in Afghanistan, I could not believe I was there. It made sense that my doctor mother should go, but what could I do in a war-torn nation? I did not go for vacation or to skip school, and I worked hard to make up the school I missed. I came because God called. I did not know how the art therapy would work. I knew God wanted me there for His purpose, so I followed Him.

As I worked with those kids, I felt that God does care about them. These children had so much taken from them: their homes, families, country. But God loves them. I realized why I was there. God wanted to use me. He wanted to love those children through me. That was my mission. I was to show these people God's amazing love and hope.

**Rebekah, preparing for service**

Perhaps the precedent that most clearly illustrates the power of listening on the advance of God's mission on earth was at the beginning of the first century. God used three inquiries. First, He sent two angels to facilitate the "empty tomb focus group," comprised of a few women who had come on the first Easter morning to find an empty tomb. While they were standing at the tomb in amazement, when they did not find the body of the Lord, "suddenly two men in dazzling clothes stood beside them" (Luke 24:4). These were messengers sent from God to act as the group facilitators. They posed the question: "Why do you look for the living among the dead?" (Luke 24:5). In the course of the discussion it was revealed to the women that He was not there, but has risen! (Luke 24:7). The women reported to the other followers of Jesus what they had learned. Peter was mobilized to find out for himself.

The Empty Tomb is immediately followed up in the Lucan account by another focus group inquiry, which could be called the "Emmaus Road Focus Group Inquiry." This time the facilitator of the discussion between the two disciples is none other than the resurrected Lord, though He initially went unrecognized. Jesus intervened in the discussion with three questions: "What are you discussing with each other while you walk along?... What things?" (Luke 24:17, 19). This second question caused the disciples to report on the incident related to the Empty Tomb Focus Group:

Some women of our group astounded us. They were at the tomb early this morning, and when they did not find His body there, they came back and told us that they had indeed seen a vision of angels who said that He was alive. Some of those who were with us went to the tomb and found it just as the women had said; but they did not see Him. (Luke 24:22-24)

The response of the two disciples led Jesus to rebuke them and pose His final question: "Oh, how foolish you are, and how slow of heart to believe all that the prophets have declared! Was it not necessary that the Messiah should suffer these things and then enter His glory?" (Luke 24:25-26). The follow-up focus group inquiry resulted in the two remaining disciples turning around and joining the other disciples already assembled in Jerusalem, where Jesus then appeared to all of them for a three-question inquiry just prior to commissioning them for the task of world evangelization. The three post-resurrection inquiries recorded sequentially in Luke 24 sparked the launch of one of the greatest advances in world evangelization in church history. Historical and biblical precedent underscore the potential of an inquiry process leading to the advance of the mission of God.

# Purpose

The purpose of the World Inquiry was to listen, to hear, and look for expressions of the mission Dei (the mission of God). In using the term "mission Dei," the emphasis was on the perfectly pure motive and essence of the mission of God, or that which finds its root and foundation in the character of God. We sought to listen to what God is doing and saying by collecting insights, beliefs, and attitudes with regard to:

*The people and the programs God is using;*

*The challenges to God's mission via factors external to the Church;*

*The obstacles internal to the Church;*

*What God is calling us to as the Body of Christ;*

*What services a global structure committed to world evangelization can offer;*

*The identification of a compelling, unifying paradigm; And, the identification of emerging leaders, and of streams of Church and mission.*

# People to Be Listened To

The emergence of Christian leadership in Africa, Asia, and Latin America, combined with the initiative toward world evangelization efforts over the last twenty-five years of the twentieth century from these regions, demanded that their ideas help shape the direction of the world evangelization in the twenty-first century. It is clear that many wish to do so; the question is how to help catalyze the true reflective inputs and resultant directions.

One of the major trends is the shift in geographical and vital center of gravity of the Church from the West and North to the East and South. Out of this new spiritual nerve center, initiative for world mission has grown exponentially. As Christianity has globalized, indigenous missions have sprung up around the world. The Christian mission and Church leaders from all around the world express their view of what the "Spirit is saying to the church" at this time. However, more than ever before that expression is coming from Asia, Africa, and Latin America:

> Since the Christian majority is now to be found outside the West and missionary initiatives from the churches of Asia, Africa, and Latin America are at the cutting-edge of the Christian world mission we must ask: What kind of theology of mission will best serve the global Christian mission in the future? What fresh theological resources can be brought to bear on this new phase of the Christian mission (Shenk 2001:98).

Jonathan Bonk expressed his concern that the focus groups for this Inquiry include a strong participation from those outside the West:

> My chief concern is that the focus groups not be simply another gathering of Western missionaries and mission executives – those whose financial means permit them

and their organizations the luxury of participation in the meetings of such focus groups ... often in venues beyond the means of 99% of the servants of God who actually incarnate the gospel to the ends of the earth! I hope that the focus groups resulting from your vision will break the mold (Bonk 2001).

The active participation of Christian leaders from the world in shaping twenty-first century world evangelization initiatives is crucial for this World Inquiry. As of June 1, 2004, 6,685 Christian church and mission leaders from more than 850 cities have participated in 111 separate World Inquiry events. Of the total involved, 6,130 people were from the Majority World, and 555 people were from North America and Western Europe.

We were watching to see whether a fresh missiology would emerge that both deepened and extended our witness through the gospel. We prayed that information might mesh with relationships of the broader world community to foster increased evangelization so that there can be a significant advance in the Christian movement over the next quarter-century.

As we purposed to listen to God primarily through the voices from the Majority World, we became aware that listening is not an end in itself as we reflected on the biblical connotation but rather the means to the end of taking responsive action (1 Corinthians 14:21). The root word *akouo* – usually translated "hear," "hearken," or "listen" – is closely related to the word *hupakouo*, which is made up of two words, *hupa* which means "under" and *akouo* which means "to hear," thus meaning "to obey." Real listening leads to obedience and action. Is it time for the Church in the West not only to listen to the voices of God's servants from the Majority World but also to act upon what they hear?

# Paradigm Emerging

At the World Inquiry International Coalition preliminary findings event in Seoul in May 2003, Mission as Transformation emerged as a new, compelling, and unifying paradigm at the beginning of the twenty-first century.

Mission as Transformation is built upon four foundational pillars of truth. First, we are living in a fallen, deformed world needing to be transformed; second, individuals are being called to be conformed to the image of Christ; third, churches are being challenged to be renewed and reformed to align with God's greater purposes; and fourth, cities, communities, peoples, and nations are being transformed.

This brings us to the question: What is transformation? There are several descriptions and various expressions of what transformation is all about. Each description emphasizes certain aspects of transformation which are often associated with one of the five major streams. The full essence of transformation incorporates personal, corporate, and societal dimensions.

# Five Major Transformational Streams

Five major, diverse transformational streams are flowing across the world and converge into the same "transformational river."

1. The *Revivalist Stream* places emphasis on divine visitation and revival. God acts on the Church bringing revival, and He acts on society bringing spiritual awakening.
2. The *Church Growth Stream* is characterized by saturation church-planting movements working in a spirit of cooperation, resulting in healthy churches in every class and kind of people, and within practical and relational reach of

every person – permeating every segment of society with the love, truth, and saving power of Jesus Christ.

3. The *City-reaching Stream* means obedience to God as an apostolic people with an apostolic mission to transform people, places, and the culture within which the Church lives.

4. The *Stream of Transformational Development of the Poor* through community development involves creating a better future for the poor.

5. There is also a *Marketplace Redemption Stream*. The marketplace – the combination business, education, and government – constitutes the heart of a nation. To be transformed, the marketplace must be transformed. An important key for the Kingdom of God to use the marketplace is found in Jesus' parable of the pounds (Luke 19:10-27) where believers are instructed to use business to gain authority over cities by using Kingdom principles.

An effort to define a comprehensive approach to transformation must be "rooted in the theology of the mission of the Kingdom of God and seeks to express the Lordship of Jesus over every aspect of life: economic, religious, personal, and political. It does not give priority to any area of life as an area for mission .... but this change will be effected whenever people address issues of life directly, rooted in a gospel perspective" (Vinay and Sugden 1999).

Transformation associates are now gathering to contemplate, then seek to cooperate with the beauty of God's movements. The basic idea behind "transformation coordination" is that, not only can we do more together than we can separately, but we move to a new ministry realm which operates on entirely new godly laws of input and output. Like the gushing forth of the waters, the love of God through the people of God unleashes multiple mission initiatives in which divine resources are channeled through willing servants to meet human needs to the glory of God.

E. Stanley Jones, missionary to India, describes the principles on which he based his public meetings with Hindus and Muslims in the 1920s.

Be absolutely frank. There should be no camouflage in hiding one's meaning or purpose by non-committal subjects. The audience must know exactly what it is coming to hear.

Announce beforehand that there is to be no attack upon anyone's religion. If there is any attack, it must be by the positive presentation of Christ. He must Himself be the attack. He would judge both of us, saving us from feelings and attitudes of superiority, so ruinous to Christian work.

Allow the audience to ask questions at the close. Face everything and dodge no difficulties. Get leading non-Christians of the city where the meetings are held to become chairmen of the meetings.

Christianity must be defined as Christ, not the Old Testament, not Western civilization, not even the system built around Him in the West, but as Christ Himself. To be a Christian is to follow Him.

Christ must be interpreted in terms of Christian experience rather than through mere argument.

Drop the word "Christianity" from any announcements. (It isn't found in the Scriptures, is it?)

Christ must be in an Indian setting. He must be the Christ of the Indian Road.

**Ashley, serving in Thailand**

A comprehensive movement to bless the nations includes many emphases. Mission initiative among the last and the least prioritizes the spiritually needy while integrating the physically needy without leaving any country out of focus. Transformational leadership engages a new generation in expanding participatory leadership with current leadership.

A transformed world is a place where the power, the presence, and the peace of God are experienced by all. The power of God is unleashed. The peace of God rules. Shalom and Salaam embrace. The presence of God fills the earth. "Steadfast love and faithfulness will meet; righteousness and peace will kiss each other. Faithfulness will spring up from the ground, and righteousness will look down from the sky" (Psalm 85:10-11).

And so collaboration builds the bridge between the act of listening and the resultant paradigm of "mission as transformation." The power of listening is demonstrated on this journey as it leads us to mission Dei. For what has greater power than the mission of God in our world today?

# Conclusion

Does collaboration have a future? Yes it does, but it calls us to journey together in a Spirit-filled listening mode. How do we reflect a servant spirit that mirrors unity in diversity as we faithfully embrace our calling together to God's mission? One way is by intentionally listening to one another. As we listen we can begin to see that the word transformation and its cognates have emerged as an expression of mission throughout the Christian world today.

Yes, there is power in listening. Let us take the practical counsel of James when he wrote: "My beloved: let everyone be quick to listen" (James 1:19).

# References Cited

Allesandra, Tony
    1995     "The Power of Listening." *Speakers Platform.*
            May 18,2004 http://speaking.com/articles_html/
            Tony Alessandra, Ph.D.,CSP,CPAE_107.html.

American Society of Missiology
    2004     "Collaboration: The Missing Link in the World
            Christian Mission." June 18-20. Annual
            Meeting. Techny, IL.

Barrett, David and Todd Johnson (eds.)
    2000     *World Christian Encyclopedia.* Oxford: Oxford
            University Press.

Bonk, Jonathan
    2001     "Evangelizing our World Inquiry." personal
            email. (September 2, 2001).

Bosch, David
    1984     *Witness to the World: The Christian Mission in
            Theological Perspective.* Atlanta: John Knox Press.

Chambers, Robert
    1988     Poverty in India: Concepts, Research and
            Reality. Sussex: Institute of Development Studies.

Christian, Jayakumar
    1999     God of the Empty-Handed: Poverty, Power and
            the Kingdom of God. Monrovia: MARC

Drucker, Peter
    1993     Post-Capitalist Society. New York: Harper and Collins.

*Economist*
    1999     "Making Money Out of Angola." 18 Sept.

Friedman, John
    1992     *Empowerment: The Politics of Development.*
            Cambridge: Blackwell.

Green, Edward
    2003     "Faith-Based Organizations: Contributions to
            HIV Prevention." *Report by the Synergy
            Project for USAID.* September.

Jayakaran, Ravi
 1999 "Holistic Participatory Learning and Action,"
  in *Working with the Poor: New Insights and
  Learnings from Development Practitioners*,
  edited by Bryant Myers.  Monrovia: MARC.

Lewis, Stephen
 2000 "Vulnerability of the Girl Child to HIV/AIDS."
  London: UK NGO AIDS Consortium.

Loewen, Jacob A.
 2000 *The Bible in Cross-Cultural Perspective*.
  Pasadena: William Carey Library.

McGavran, Donald
 1970 *Understanding Church Growth*.  Grand Rapids:
  Wm. B. Eerdmans Pub. Co.

McKaughan, Paul
 2000 personal email.  (August 21, 2000).

McKaughan, Paul, Dellana O'Brien, and William O'Brien
 1989 *Choosing a Future for U.S. Missions*.  Monrovia.
  MARC.

Myers, Bryant L.
 2000a "The New Context of  World Mission," in *Mission
  Handbook: U.S. and Canadian Christian Ministries
  Overseas*, edited by John A. Siewert and Edna G.
  Valdez.  Monrovia: MARC.

 2000b *Walking with the Poor: Principles and Practice
  of Transformational Development*.  Maryknoll:
  Orbis Books.

 2003 *Exploring World Mission*.  Monrovia: World Vision.

Neill, Stephen
 1959 *Creative Tension*.  London: Edinburgh House Press.

 1984 "How My Mind has Changed About Mission."
  3 part video series taped at the Overseas Ministries
  Study Center, Atlanta.  Southern
  Baptist Convention.

Newbigin, Lesslie
    1978     *The Open Secret: Sketches for a Missionary Theology*. Grand Rapids: Wm. B. Eerdmans Pub. Co.

Shenk, Wilbert R.
    2001     "Recasting Theology of Mission: Impulses from the Non-Western World." *International Bulletin of Missionary Research*. 25:3:98-107.

Smith, Donald K.
    1992     *Creating Understanding*. Grand Rapids: Zondervan.

Stott, John R.
    2001     *Christian Mission in the Modern World*. Downers Grove: InterVarsity Press.

Thurman, Sandra
    2000     "The Director of the Office of National AIDS Policy at the White House." *East African Standard*. (24 January).

UNAIDS
    2004     "Report on the Global AIDS Epidemic." United Nations Fact sheet.

Verkuyl, Johannes
    1978     *Contemporary Missiology: An Introduction*. Grand Rapids: Wm. B. Eerdmans Pub. Co.

Vinay, Samuel and Chris Sudgen (eds.)
    1999     *Mission as Transformation: A Theology of the Whole Gospel*. Oxford: Regnum.

Go to the people, Live with them.
Learn from them.
Start with what they know, Build with what they have,
But with the best leaders.
When the work is done, The task accomplished,
The people will say, "We have done it ourselves."

**Lao Tsu —300 BC**

# 4
# What Would Jesus Do About Poverty?

by Ashley Barker

## "Come, Follow Me"

If the rich young ruler could obey Jesus' command to "go" and then "give all to the poor" he would be in a place to follow Jesus. He would not be left destitute. He would join a community that was living out true faith in Christ, helping to establish the Kingdom of God on earth.

We must be clear about joining Jesus' community. Jesus preached, delivered, healed and gave the message of the Kingdom. Jesus' central concern was not socializing people into His church, but proclaiming the reign of God and seeing its authority heal and restore the most vulnerable. "Repent, for the Kingdom of God has come near." (Matthew 4:17). There are 114 references to "God's reign" in Matthew, Mark, and Luke alone but "church" is only mentioned four times (and all in Matthew, and three times in one chapter (18) relating to resolving conflict). If we are to join Jesus we must be prepared "to seek first the Kingdom of God and its justice" above all other agendas. Proclaiming the reign of God was Jesus' purpose, a foundation for everything else, and it must be ours too if we are to be faithful to Christ. Unfortunately the term "Kingdom of God" has become so clichéd and domesticated it has lost most of its radical meaning. What then is the nature of this reign and what has it to do with responding to poverty?

The Hebrew understanding of poverty is much broader than destitution. It would be tempting to conclude that poverty is simply powerlessness. The Hebrew people were oppressed in all kinds of ways because they did not have power. It could follow then that the answer to poverty is to give the poor lots of power. Certainly many contemporary development workers define poverty in such terms.

The theme of poverty as powerlessness is right, but only to a point. There is a difference between power and true authority. The latter is being true to who God has made us to be and true to what we are given to do in God's world. Those in poverty then do not have the "authority" to live the full, healthy and meaningful lives God intends for them. Simply gaining power, status or wealth then are shallow answers to the deep problems faced by the poor. In post-colonial times in countries such as Cambodia, Vietnam and Burma, simply gaining power (over and above others) just replaced one set of oppressors with another. What Jesus proclaimed and offered was authority to live as God intends.

As Christians we believe Jesus is the hope of shalom realized – the ultimate revelation of what God intends. He is the Lord of *shalom* (2 Thessalonians 3:16) and is anointed to bring "good news for the poor" (Luke 4:18-19), fulfilling all the laws, including the Jubilee laws. Jesus is the "anchor of the soul" and the hope of our faith (Hebrews 6:19). Jesus could do this for us because He did not give into temptation, even under persecution, torture and execution. Therefore only Jesus had the authority to choose real life and sacrificial death and could offer this life, through His resurrection and the Spirit to others. The disciples received this grace freely and could then go and offer Jesus' authority and life to others. "Jesus is Lord" then became an early faith statement proclaiming the reality that Jesus' authority was above all others and that our own authority and freedom to live as God intends was linked intrinsically with this authentic authority and freedom.

The reign of God then is about the Lordship of Christ, or the shalom of God breaking through. Jesus' authority was shown then whenever Jesus was in the midst of people, when demons were cast out and when healing and miracles in nature occurred. Jesus' teaching about this reign were often parables set in homes, marketplaces or on the land, requiring us to risk all against anti-reigns in "seeking first the reign of God and its justice." Jesus is the center and reference point of this reign of God. Jesus turns upside down the centers and reference points of those who only have power and not authority. This is what made Jesus' life so threatening. God could have entered our world as Jesus at anytime, anywhere, so we must pay attention to how Jesus chose to live. If Jesus is the reference point of God's reign, then we need to conform to Jesus' life and image.

## Jesus Experienced Poverty Personally
Jesus was conceived out of wedlock. He fled persecution as a refugee to Egypt. He lived in an oppressed land as part of an oppressed people at the hands of the colonizing Romans. Jesus experienced hunger (Matthew 12) and hopelessness (Matthew 8:20). Jesus was discriminated against by both Romans and other Jews because He was from Nazareth. He was tortured, falsely tried and murdered.

## Jesus Taught Insights that Offered Authority to Transform Poverty to be like Heaven and Earth
Jesus prayed for God's reign to come here on earth as in Heaven. Jesus warned of a final day where the sheep and goats will be separated according to how they treated the "least

of these." The goats included people like the rich man who ignored the beggar, and the rich fool who stored up wealth. Jesus explained the lure of wealth was like weeds that choked the seed. Jesus cursed the rich and blessed the poor, but offered a Kingdom community life where labels of rich and poor were not allowed. Jesus promised His presence to "be with" those who "go" and seek disciples of this Kingdom coming.

## Jesus Demonstrated the Kingdom's Coming Through Miracles

Jesus personally touched lepers and "unclean" women and made them whole again. He healed the blind on the Sabbath. He enabled enough loaves and fish to multiply to feed multitudes after His disciples gave what little they had to feed the hungry. He cast out oppressive evil spirits in people – often children, women or those on the "other side" of society.

## Jesus Empowered Christian Communities to Live like Him by Dying, Rising Again and Giving Us His Spirit

Jesus showed that sacrifice until death is required to beat oppression. He showed by example how to live with others. He rose again from the dead as evidence of God's pleasure of His life. His Spirit was given so that all people, poor and non-poor alike, could continue His mission in the world and end poverty. Jesus' early church did this so well that "they were all together and no one was in need."

## Jesus Warned that the "End of the Age" Would Come

How people respond or do not respond to "the least of these" (sick, homeless, hungry, jailed) is the litmus test of where we place our faith. Is our faith and trust in Jesus and His reign's authority or is it in the world's power? (Matthew 25:31ff).

Each morning Alumetu, my language helper, and I pray that God will open our eyes to the opportunities that God has planned in advance for us. Each day something new comes about, and I confess that sometimes I wonder if it is from God.

One day as I sat outside studying Amharic and enjoying the afternoon, a soccer ball came over the compound wall -- a regular occurrence because there is an open lot next to my compound. I looked at the soccer ball, which was half flat and had more rips and tears in it than any ball I had ever seen. In America we would have thrown it away a long time ago. But soccer is the national sport of Ethiopia, and all the children love to play. When there is not enough money for food, they cannot afford to throw a soccer ball away even when it has had its day on the field. The boys came to the gate and got the ball.

That day I wondered, "Is God trying to speak to me through this soccer ball?" Seriously, I thought there was no way. But the boys kept kicking this ball over the fence. I would not have thought too much about it, but it seemed as if the ball continued to land right in front of me. Next, I wondered  how much a new soccer ball would cost, so I asked my friend Fikadu. He was not sure, but he went to find out. He came back and said the ball would cost 16 birr -- that's less than two dollars since 8.6 birr equals one dollar. This wasn't a real leather soccer ball, but a rubber one. A good leather soccer ball costs 140 birr, about $16.50, more than most people in this area make in an entire month.

The weekend was coming so I decided to buy a new ball, then wait for the ball to come over the wall again and see what would happen.

I waited on Saturday, but no ball. Late Sunday afternoon while I sat outside practicing language with Alumetu, the ball came over the wall. We waited, and the boys came to the gate. Fikadu answered the gate, then the boys asked for their ball. He told them no they could not have it. One boy pulled out a birr asking for the ball. Again, he told them "No," and asked the boy who owned the ball to come into the compound. You could tell he was a little scared, but he stood there looking at his ball. I told him to wait, ran into the house, and came out with the new ball. I told him I was keeping the old one. He backed up all the way to the gate saying "Oh, thank you. Oh, thank you!" Outside the gate, the boys gave a victory yell similar to the one that the women at church use to praise God. I cannot even describe the sound, so you will just have to use your imagination.

Feeling pretty good about what I did, I thanked God and went on thinking that was it. Ha! God had a bigger plan that had not been revealed; this was merely the beginning. I received a letter in broken English with all of the boys' names signed to it thanking me for the ball. They also wanted to know if I would sponsor their team. What had I gotten myself into? I thought, "Okay, God, this is something I need to share with one of the leaders at the church because this would be a real challenge." I say challenge because while I watched the boys play one day, one of them got mad at another player and pulled a knife on him.

I was not aware that we had a sports minister at our church in Addis Ababa, but as I spoke to the church leader he said he would introduce me to him so that we could possibly help these boys. None of these boys attended our church. Most of the boys come from families who are Orthodox, Muslim, Catholic, or animist. The sports minister, Hailyesus, he said he would meet with the boys to see if they were really serious. Hailyesus has 11 other soccer teams, and, for the most part, all of them attend the church. This would be an outreach like no other. Hailyesus was excited about the possibilities. The boys came to practice one Friday afternoon to show their stuff, and they were good. They needed discipline and a coach willing to work with them. I took a team picture of them and printed one off for Hailyesus. He told me that most of the guys were gangsters! I began to question God about what He had gotten me into.

Hailyesus said he wanted me to help with these boys and the ministry. Again I began questioning God, since I have no clue about soccer or sports ministry, or about teenage boys. I began to pray for the boys, all eighteen of them. I prayed that God would show me how I was to be a part of these boys' lives and the sports ministry.

Ethiopians are very hospitable, and sharing food and fellowship is very important in building relationships. Knowing this, I began to think of ways I could show Christ to these boys. God gave me the answer through the Easter holiday, which was May 1 for the Ethiopian people. I had a copy of the movie, The Passion of the Christ, and intended to use it for the church and evangelism. I did not know I would get to use it so soon. Because there are so many Muslims in Ethiopia, Mohammed's birthday is celebrated and the students all get out of school that day. I thought that this might be a good night to show the film. One of the leaders advised me to put all of my things away so nothing would get stolen. I decided I would trust God instead and invited all eighteen of them to my house.

They all showed up ready to watch the film. Because they may have not been interested in a religious film, I gave them several questions to think about while watching the film. For example: Who were the good and bad teams in the movie? And Who won the game in the end? Needless to say, they all wanted to answer the questions. Hailyesus left with the boys, and three of them asked him "Did Jesus really die like this for us?" The seeds have been planted. God is so good!

**Shelly, serving in Ethiopia**

# The Impact of the Early Church on Poverty

The Way personified by Jesus, His first community and the early church movement worked. It was able to survive and thrive even though Jesus was with them in a different way after His execution.

> Now the whole group of those who believed were of one heart and soul, and no one claimed private ownership of any possessions, but everything they owned was held in common. With great power the apostles gave their testimony to the resurrection of the Lord Jesus, and great grace was upon them all. There was not a needy person among them, for as many as owned land or houses sold them and brought the proceeds of what was old. They laid it at the apostles' feet, and it was distributed to each as any had need (Acts 4:32-35).

There was not a needy person among them! Such was the Jesus movement that poverty was ended in a movement made up of many needy people. The Christian response to poverty then can be varied. Consider that Jesus and the early church:

- *gave a fish* – as when they responded to direct needs through healing or feeding the hungry. Today we would call this "relief", which includes responses such as feeding programs, emergency development, health care, prayer, providing accommodation and visitation of those who are in jail or sick.
- *taught how to fish* – as when they taught truths for people such as Zacchaeus to put into practice. Today we would call this "education", which includes responses such as job creation, preventative medical

care, teaching literacy and numeracy and vocational training.

- *asked why there was no fish* – as Jesus did when He turned the tables upside down in the temple or the apostles did when they confronted rulers and crowds who were oppressing people. Today we would call this "protest and advocacy," which includes addressing political systems, campaigning and changing laws that create poverty and oppression. Advocating population control and secure land tenure and fighting unjust economic structures could be included here.

- *modeled a new way to fish* – as Jesus did when He became a human, forming an apostolic community living in solidarity, fleshing out good news with those in need. The apostles lived similarly, serving in weakness. This could be called "incarnational modeling," which could include responses such as Christians relocating to live among needy neighborhoods, the starting of neighborhood churches of the people and life-on-life discipleship with those in need.

- *saw a new way to fish owned by the people* – as Jesus and the apostles did when they so empowered a local movement it could live on without them physically there. Today we would call this "transformation," which could include neighborhood transformations, church planting movements of the poor and grassroots political cells.

Responding to poverty with relief or education can give us places to start in addressing poverty. Each response is pleasing to God in its own right and can help move toward freedom from oppression. If these responses are to be like Christ's and the early church they cannot just be "bait" to catch fish with though. God wants to help restore the image of God in people, regardless of whether they acknowledge him or not.

Responses to poverty then are not simply a "means" to the "end" of conversion or church growth.

If our responses are not genuine the people will know it. The poor might "play the game" for a while -- "rice Christians" might even be made – but the deep-seated feelings of exploitation and resentment will be harder to shake. Credibility for Christ in the community might even be permanently damaged for some. Different kinds of responses to poverty can be blessed by God if it is done at the right time, in the right way and with the right motivations. We know this because Jesus and the early church did all these. Yet if we ask, "Which of these responses to poverty do today's churches use most and least, if they do get involved with the poor?" we are faced with some embarrassing answers. Despite the fact that Jesus and the early church did all these things, too often Christians are not prepared to go past relief. Why?

Perhaps the call to live among the poor to see a liberating Christian neighborhood movement is simply more costly and less sexy. It is one thing to feed the hungry, it is another to go to jail defending people's right to eat. In relief we can feel good about giving, but by transformation we have far more at stake than spare cash. It is hard to go past power as a motivation to stay in relief. In relief we are totally in control. By the time we see a transforming movement emerge we who may initiate it are out of control.

The body of Christ has something unique to offer the world in the last two responses. Jesus and the apostolic bands showed a new way to fish, to be taken on by the poor and those in solidarity with the poor. Neighborhoods can gather together as a social movement to end poverty as we know it by following Jesus in the authority of the Holy Spirit.

Some of the biggest thrills I have had in mission are seeing pilot projects or new churches taken over by those who were helped by it. It is always a thrill for me to visit the Emmanuel Fellowship which meets in a Scout hall in a suburb of Melbourne. When I see Simon preaching and leading the fellowship, I get a buzz. It brings back memories of when Simon was struggling and we would go fishing and talk about life and pray and dream. Seeing converts run churches – no longer needing you and in fact challenging and ministering to you – warms my heart like nothing else does.

Yet, with the transformation of others came lack of control for me. The sentiment of having trouble letting go is a very real temptation. Especially if converts run things in a way that makes me cringe. Given that communities facing poverty often struggle to analyze their situations, I find it hard to shut up and allow the people to go through the process of learning without my input. When a church is autonomous from us we can only dialogue and not order. Our authority is more prophetic and medicine-man like, than structural and chief like. God has made these local leaders responsible for the project or church after all and not me. We have to trust that the Bible and Holy Spirit can guide them as they have guided us. This is not foolproof, but it is promoting maturity, and allowing a true movement of the people emerge that can be God's answer to the cries of their heart.

Almost the first thing that happens to those who are being transformed is a kind of independence. Input soon comes from elsewhere. This natural kind of maturing process – not unlike adolescence – is crucial if we are to work ourselves out of a job. Sure, they will make wrong calls. Yet, it is better for them to make the wrong calls than those non-indigenous people to the community making the wrong calls. Ultimately, non-indigenous people can choose to walk away. Indigenous people do not have such powers. It is crucial therefore that we aim to have the new way to fish owned by the people.

While we may start with relief, we cannot end there. What would Jesus do about poverty? He would take seriously every possible response in seeing the Good News proclaimed to and with the poor, especially seeing distinctly Christian movements stand against poverty together.

> Do not stretch your hands
> out to heaven but rather
> to the poor.
> John Chrysostom

# 5

# Compassion With an Attitude: A Humanitarian's View of Human Suffering

by Bryant L. Myers

This chapter provides a perspective on human suffering through the humanitarian's lens afforded by my experience working for a large relief and development organization. Sadly, there is much suffering to survey. A comprehensive review exceeds the bounds of this essay, but I will provide capsule updates on the status of three particularly vulnerable groups in today's world: children, refugees, and those with HIV/AIDS. There will not be very much good news; the world is not a hospitable place for so many of its citizens.

The paper will then move to a reflection on biblical compassion, what I will call compassion with an attitude. I want to suggest an understanding of compassion that not only cares but also challenges, a compassion that insists that the causes of suffering, not just the symptoms, must be addressed.

# Children

There are a lot of children in the world. When we walk down the street in the West, we do not often realize this, since only one in five of the people we see are under the age of 15.

In the Third World, it is estimated that 30 to 40% of the population is under the age of 15.

The world is not a nurturing place for many of the world's children. Put simply, it is hard to grow up when you are poor, marginalized, and forgotten. Health services are few; eleven million children die every year from diseases that we routinely prevent in the West. Over one billion children do not have access to schools. The schools that do exist are poor and costly to attend. Girls are far less likely to go to school than boys.

Over 250 million children have to work instead of going to school. Bonded labor disappeared in Europe hundreds of years ago, yet earlier this year in India I met a young man named David who rolls cigarettes 10 hours a day, six days a week. David faces four years of bonded labor in order to pay back a $35 loan his parents took out for the wedding of his sister — four years of labor for the cost of taking my family out to dinner.

The world is not a safe place for children. 100 million children live on the streets of the world's cities, a world of drugs, crime, and abuse. Physical and sexual abuse damage over 625 million of the world's children. It is estimated that almost 6 million children fall prey to pedophiles every year. Three hundred thousand boys and girls have been forcibly made into child soldiers (Barrett and Johnson, 2000:6).

Sometimes I don't get Paul. He once wrote, "How beautiful are the feet of those who bring Good News!" (Romans 10:15). I mean, take a look at my feet! What kind of news must I be bringing?

Nearly everyone here in Klong Toey slum has feet like mine. Over time the combination of flip-flops on hot concrete transforms even the softest hoofs into gross monsters able to scare small children at a single glance. Feet are a tell-all sign of poverty here. If we ever go out of the slum with neighbors, say to a movie, it feels like people are staring down and thinking, "Yeah, wear your best shirt if you like, but shuffling along on those flaky feet tells us exactly where you are from."

Compare our feet to the office workers, who rarely touch plastic and concrete as they get out of their air-conditioned offices into their air-conditioned cars and back to their air-conditioned homes. Though it is 95 degrees outside, they all probably wear socks all day and night! Some even get professionals to massage, groom and make their feet smell sweet!

I am encouraged though that Jesus probably did not have beautiful, sweet-smelling feet. Other than a borrowed donkey, He walked those dusty, dirty first-century Palestine streets on His speaking and healing tours. Certainly the disciples did not line up to take turns to wash each others' feet at the end of a long day's journey. Jesus' rough feet are finally disfigured by having a nail hammered through them. Not the kind of feet to show off down at the beach club.

Had Jesus lived like a televangelist on tour in the best private jets and swanky hotels he would have had nice feet, but bugger all Good News for the poor. It was because His feet took Him to the tough places, showing a new way to live that the Good News came. There is no other way to bring the Gospel than to enflesh it. Jesus' life, death and resurrection made the Good News real for the poor and His fleshy feet would have shown the marks.

If Jesus did not have beautiful feet, neither did Paul. They lived remarkably tough lives, but brought ultimate Good News. What is this verse about feet really mean then? The Greek word gives us a clue. Translated as "beautiful" is horairias, which is actually closer in meaning to our word "timely" or the "right season" than "beautiful" or "extremely good looking." It comes from the root that means "hour." The verse then is about feet bringing timely news, which in turn has an eternal beauty.

While my wife is beautiful in every sense, we have struggled to make our home in Klong Toey beautiful in every way. Anji wrote about this:

> Over the time we have been here in the slum I have been slowly fixing things up, or so I thought, to make the place more livable. When Aiden was 4 months old we made a kind of kids bedroom and put in a small air-conditioner. To keep the air we had to block up many holes in the walls and windows, initially with plastic bags and then eventually with wood. Well, I thought I was pretty clever. Covering up the holes also meant a reduction in the number of mosquitoes that could get in. However, I was soon to learn that many problems that look easy to solve here in the slum are not that simple!

> Our house began to constantly stink like a public toilet! Ash's conclusion was, "It's a slum. Everything smells." I, however, was quite disconcerted that our house seemed to smell more than the outside sewer. I went on a mission with sprays and cleaning products, as well as poisons to kill that various vermin that I suspected to be causing the strong smell. Well, nothing worked.

> Then a month before we left for Australia, urine started leaking through the ceiling. One morning I was settled down to enjoy my morning cuppa, when wee started dripping through the roof into the kettle and splashing into my bowl of cereal. I decided that this rat was a goner! We set traps and caught a number of rather large rats before leaving.

> After returning from Australia, I started to notice a really strong smell around 3 am each morning, and then one day I woke up to a yellow puddle, much of which

splashed into my nearby handbag! Hoping to set a rat trap upstairs, I asked our neighbor to help me with a light, which had broken. He pulled back the plastic sheet used to cover the rough wooden floor and we found the wood completely soaked with urine. He determined that a rat could not make such a large quantity, so it must be human! Now I was ready to throw my kettle out.

Over the next few days his sister-in-law, who lives in one of the four rooms upstairs decided to keep a look out for the culprit. After two more puddles of urine, we discovered the 3 am wee-er – a frail old man who could not manage the stairs down to the toilet very well at night.

Well, now he has a bucket which we have offered to empty each morning if he promises not to keep weeing on the floor! I plan to soon to start to open up some of the holes in the walls with the hope that the airflow will help reduce the stink of urine-soaked rotting wood.

Anyway, it got me thinking about so many of the issues that we see in the slum, that look so easy to fix, but often leave us baffled as to why things are the way they are. I can be so guilty of rushing in with a quick fix that may just make things smell worse in the end! I pray that God will guide us as we try to listen more than talk, understand more than being understood, and work together with, rather than for the poor in this community.

In a world of a billion urban slum-dwellers, should timely feet end up ugly feet? Does it matter if our house does not make the front cover of Better Homes and Gardens? What becomes ugly now for the sake of the Gospel – from poverty, hardship, crossing barriers – has a real kind of beauty for doing what counts for eternity. Is it now the case that the uglier our feet the better the news for us and a hurting, concrete-clad world?

By 2025 there will be two billion urban slum-dwellers, so we could do with a few more Christian feet getting ugly to bring Good News. Come on ugly feet, keep walking!

**Ashley, serving in Thailand**

Earlier this year, our son James surprised us by going to Uganda to work as a volunteer in a home for abandoned babies. It was a tough immersion for this privileged 19-year-old. Finding babies abandoned in latrines, cooking the children's meals on open fires outside the simple building that housed the babies, coping with very limited healthcare — James thought he had seen it all. Then he went to Gulu in the north, to a reception center for child soldiers who had escaped the Lord's Resistance Army. Children traumatized by war, turned into killers, missing lips and noses.

# The Uprooted

Too many people on our planet are not living at home. Conflict, disasters, and environmental collapse have dramatically increased the number of refugees from 2.5 million in 1975 to almost 12 million in 2003 (although it is pleasing to note that this is down from a high of 27 million in 1995). To this tally, however, one must add the almost 24 million internally displaced people who have migrated to another part of their own country, fleeing conflict and persecution. The vast majority of these refugees are women and children. Over 65 percent are Muslim.

Living as uprooted people is hard enough without then being exploited in refugee camps by those who would sustain the conflict. Diamonds, oil, drugs, and even relief aid are exploited by militias, rebels, and governments to sustain civil war. Victims are used by both sides of the conflict for legitimacy and sanctuary.

# HIV/AIDS

HIV/AIDS is the greatest humanitarian emergency of our time. It threatens the lives of millions of people and the social well-being of whole nations. Almost 40 million people are infected

When Francis was riding toward Assisi one day he saw a leper by the road. Most people at the time considered leprosy highly contagious and hid in fear when a leper crossed their path. This was Francis's first impulse. Leprosy was considered a fate worse than death and so contagious that even a glance could pass the disease. But on that morning a taboo would be broken.

That morning in prayer, God had impressed upon Francis that what society says people need to make them happy is not what gives real joy -- and that the reign of God begins precisely among those of whom society is most afraid. The Legend of the Three Companions tells us that Francis "had always felt an overpowering horror of these sufferers, but making a great effort, he conquered his aversion, dismounted and, in giving the leper a coin, kissed his hand." Overwhelmed by Francis's act of compassion, the leper gave Francis a kiss of peace in return. Francis had humanized a person once thought of as less than human. He had become more humanized by touching another person. Lepers would become of special concern to Francis and he would nurse lepers the rest of his life.

Francis died prematurely at about the age of 44, almost certainly of tuberculoid leprosy. Yet, blind on his death-bed, cared for by his friend Claire and her sisters, Francis wrote one of the most famous poems in history, "The Canticle of Brother Sun." Francis would have lived longer if he had not contracted leprosy, but he would not have been more alive to God and others. If he had been held captive by his society's fears of the poor, he would not have personified and fleshed out a movement that was one of God's unique answers to the cries of the poor.

**Ashley, serving in Thailand**

with the virus. In 2003, 8,000 people died every day from AIDS. During that same year, almost 100,000 a week were being infected (UNAIDS, 2004).

Over 15 million children under the age of 15 have lost their mother, their father, or both parents to AIDS. This figure is expected to double by 2010. Too many African teenagers are heads of households. Too many grandmothers are raising their grandchildren in simple homes behind which they have buried their own children. I have met some of these grandmothers — frail, weak, and exhausted, doing what needs to be done.

It is no hyperbole to say that HIV/AIDS bears all the hallmarks of the Evil One. It reveals the fractures, stresses, and strains in societies, exploring disorder, inequality, and poverty. The virus seeks out the weak, poor, and vulnerable.

HIV/AIDS disproportionately singles out women. As Stephen Lewis, the UN Special Envoy for HIV/AIDS in Africa, notes, "It goes without saying that the virus has targeted women with a raging and twisted Darwinian ferocity. It goes equally without saying that gender inequality is what sustains and nurtures the spread of the virus" (UNAIDS, 2004). Women are made vulnerable through the influence of culture and tradition, stigma and discrimination, and land rights issues.

HIV/AIDS has been raging in Africa for over 20 years while the world and most of the churches have slept. The next wave of the pandemic will be in India, China, and Russia, home to almost one-third of the world's population. We are at the beginning of the pandemic, not the middle, not the end. This is a century-long struggle.

Sadly, until just recently, the attitude of the churches, especially in the United States, has been to react as the disciples did to the blind man in John 9, asking: "Who sinned? This man or his parents?" HIV/AIDS has been seen as God's judgment for bad moral behavior. Sadly, condemnation and judgment have replaced the gospel values of grace and compassion.

Furthermore, HIV/AIDS has a horrific impact on the churches in Africa, a frequently overlooked dimension of which is the impact on pastors. I attended a meeting of pastors in Rakai, the epicenter of the pandemic in Uganda, and I have never seen a group that looked and sounded so tired and defeated. They are burying people every day of every week; the pastorate has become a burial business.

Yet, where the churches teach faithfulness and abstinence to couples and teenagers, prevalence rates have reversed. This is the case in Uganda (Green, 2003). When the churches do their job of discipleship, good things happen.

# Compassion with an Attitude

The evidence of human suffering around the world is inarguable. Whether through stories or statistics, the level of unacceptable human suffering is plain to see for those who wish to see it. But some, it seems, do not. Where are the marks of suffering on the Western church, the favored few, who are safe and secure?

Consider the story of the leper and Jesus. "A leper came to him begging him, and kneeling he said to him, 'If you choose, you can make me clean.' Moved with pity, Jesus stretched out his hand and touched him, and said to him, 'I do choose. Be made clean!' Immediately the leprosy left him, and he was made clean" (Mark 1:40-42).

Notice that immediately after the man called out, Jesus stopped and listened to him. Compassion begins with opening ourselves to awareness, seeing and hearing the needs around us. We need to see those who are in pain, who are forgotten, who are on the sidelines. We need to hear their voices calling for help, moaning in pain. Not everyone does this kind of hearing and seeing. Most stay safely away from the places where the poor live. They turn off the news when it comes to *favelas* and refugee camps. It is not that they do not care, it is that they want to avoid what they see as depressing news.

Compassion, then begins with seeing the suffering of others and being willing to listen to its call. If we are willing to see and to hear, we must next be willing to feel. The Greek word for compassion or pity is derived from the word for spleen or intestine. The text says that Jesus felt compassion, and this means that His stomach went into a knot when He saw the leper. The marring impact of leprosy on a human life wrenched His gut in a deeply visceral way. The first part of being truly and incarnationally compassionate is to be moved to the core of our being with pity and outrage when in the presence of human suffering.

To hear, see, and feel is the foundation of compassion. Yet it is not compassion itself. In its fullest sense, compassion is an action word. Driven by conviction and mercy, we must act, and act in the moment. Jesus acted — he healed the man. Likewise the Good Samaritan acted — he did not write a memo about crossing the road, but crossed the road, setting aside his timetable, ignoring his ethnicity and risking his money.

There is more. The compassionate actions that Jesus took were not simply ameliorative. Jesus did not relieve the leper's pain and move on. He healed the man and instructed him to go to the temple for ritual cleansing, to be restored to his rightful place in the community of men and women. Compassion is more than mercy, more than simple response. Biblical compassion has a bias in favor of social restoration.

Compassion is hearing and seeing, feeling strongly, and acting restoratively. Finally, there is one more important lesson to learn from Mark 1, a lesson easily missed. "Moved with pity, Jesus stretched out His hand and touched him." Jesus did not have to touch the leper to heal him. Words alone would have been enough if physical healing were all that Jesus was trying to accomplish. By touching the man, Jesus was adding a message to His compassionate act of healing.

A leper in first century Palestine was an outcast. Jewish law called for complete separation from the community. To touch a leper was to break the law. Those in positions of religious and social authority were keen to see this law upheld. This preoccupation with the letter of the law at the expense of what was good for human beings was an issue of considerable concern for Jesus. Jesus disliked seeing the law applied in a way that harmed or limited people. He went out of His way to expose this misapplication of the law, teaching that the law should be for healthy relationships and human well-being. At the end of the day, the law is about loving.

In the leper, Jesus saw more than a man whose body was marred by disease. He saw a human being rejected by the community, cast out, made wholly "other." The social identity of the leper had been marred. Jesus knew that the religious and social establishment of the day believed this exclusion was both right and required by God. Healing the leper was not enough. The deeper social sin in the minds of the religious and social leaders had to be addressed as well. Jesus' decision to touch the man was meant to add a message to his act of compassion. Touching the man was a radical critique of the dominant culture of his day. The simple act of touching the untouchable called into question the leaders of the people and their understanding of what God required.

In its fullest form, compassion is seeing, feeling, and acting in a way that poses a radical critique of the dominant voices of the day, reminding them of what God requires of them. This seemingly small story in Mark carries a significant message: The biblical Christian needs to do compassion in a way that creates a gospel commentary on the causes of human suffering. This means showing compassion to refugees, yet doing so in a

Several months ago, one of our employees —a lady who brings us water —came to me nearly in tears. The monthly wages we gave her the day before were lost. Apparently, they "fell" out of her clothing as she walked home. What was she going to do? She also wanted to know what I was going to do.

Instead of voicing my doubts about her situation, I looked around our yard and noticed my husband Kip visiting with three of the local church leaders. I walked over and greeted the men, then proceeded to explain the woman's situation. "What can we do?" I asked them. As they discussed the problem, they raised the same doubts about her story that I had, and concluded it was not their problem. Hesitantly, I asked, "What would Jesus do for her? What should we, His followers, do?" Oh, that changed things. Suddenly, they started discussing the issue from church leaders' perspectives rather than as people of the world. And their decision startled me.

"We've decided that each one of us here, including you and Kip, should give her a portion of our own money to help her," they answered. "We don't know if she is telling the truth or not, but we know that Jesus has asked us to help people who need it." We pooled our money. She had lost 1,200 Kenya shillings; we each gave her 200 shillings, totaling 1,000 shillings. Then they asked me to take it over to the lady.

I walked across the yard with our gift and sat in the dirt beside her. I explained to her, as tears formed in my eyes, what had happened: "We don't know if you are telling the truth or not, but we do know that Jesus wants us to follow Him and help those in need." As I handed her the money, in 200-shilling portions, I continued, "This is not just from Kip and me, but from Etuuny, Echom, and Losikiria, leaders of the church and followers of Jesus. We have done this to obey the words of Jesus. And now, as you take our gift, I want you to remember today. When you see someone else who needs help, remember these men and remember the lifestyle of Jesus and help that person."

Shocked, she nodded her assent and thanks, then stood up to leave. This was as new to me as it was to her. This kind of solution does not happen every day.

**Katy, serving in Kenya**

way that unmasks the human greed and hunger for power that created the conflict from which refugees flee. For example, calling for biblical compassion to the one million internally displaced people in Angola in 1999 needed to include exposing the malfeasance of the UN peacekeepers and naming the companies that were enriching themselves by helping the two sides of the war exchange diamonds and oil for guns (*Economist*, 1999).

Responding compassionately to the sick without commenting on their lack of access to healthcare or their poverty is incomplete compassion. Calling for a compassionate response to the African victims of HIV/AIDS without challenging the pricing and availability of antiretroviral drugs is truncated compassion.

Compassion without a gospel comment concerning the causes of human suffering is not biblical compassion. Depending upon the underlying issue, the commentary can be personal, like the admonition to "Go and sin no more" to the woman caught in adultery; or it can be social commentary, like touching a leper that everyone knows should not be touched. But the gospel critique is always there, beckoning us to turn around and truly enter the kingdom.

Of course, this idea of compassion with a message puts us in a pickle. Compassion that critiques the powers that be can get you hurt. Unmasking the dominant culture is dangerous to your health; indeed, it can get you nailed to a cross. Helping without a message is safer, but Jesus calls us to step out in faith.

# Conclusion:
# The Marks of an Engaged Church

What kind of marks should we look for to distinguish a Western church that has embraced "incarnational empathy"? I will suggest three signs.

## Sacrificial Giving

The first is sacrificial giving — a Good Samaritan kind of giving, the kind of giving that inconveniences us and sacrifices the daily diary, the kind of giving that not only gets a suffering man to an inn but leaves money with the innkeeper. The good news is that churches tend to be pretty good at this. The majority of charitable giving for the poor comes from communities of faith. The not-so-good news is that only a little over five percent of the monies raised by churches go to foreign missions (Barrett and Johnson, 2000:22).

## Making Noise in Powerful Places

There is a second mark for which we need to look, one associated with the attitude of compassion. This is the mark that comes from making noise in polite and powerful places, the kind of mark that comes from taking positions that are unpopular and provocative, the mark that comes from challenging conventional wisdom. This is the kind of mark that comes from reminding the rich man that a beggar sits outside his gate, and that the choice the rich man makes in response is of eternal significance.

## Prayer

Finally, the third mark on the church is prayer. To be sure, this is not the prayer that calls for merely taking suffering away. Suffering is simply a reality in our fallen world. Instead, this is the kind of prayer that begs God to take suffering, Satan's best shot at convincing us that there is no loving God, and transform it so that it reveals what Satan is so desperately trying to conceal: *a loving God who suffers with us*. We must not forget that Jesus' response to His disciple's question in John 9 was that neither the man's sins nor his parents' sins caused the blindness. Rather, this man suffered so that the glory of God could be revealed.

## References Cited

Barrett, David, George Kurian and Todd Johnson
    2000    *World Christian Encyclopedia*. Oxford: Oxford University Press.

*Economist*
    1999    "Making Money out of Angola." *Economist*. 18 Sept.

Green, Edward
    2003    "Faith-Based Organizations: Contributions to HIV Prevention." *Report of the Synergy Project of USAID*.

UNAIDS
    2004    "Report on the Global AIDS Epidemic." *United Nations Fact sheet*.

Today it is fashionable to talk about the poor. Unfortunately it is not fashionable to talk with them.

**Mother Teresa**

# 6

# Toward a Missiology of Transformation

by Charles Van Engen

Missions in the twenty-first century must undergo a radical transformation. It needs to be always the same mission: God's mission, the *missio Dei*.

## Historical Location: Setting the Stage

After World War II there was a rather severe split between differing views of Christian mission. Heavily impacted by a guilty conscience about the Holocaust and the Third Reich, the World Council of Churches stressed a theology of relevance with heavy socio-political agendas.

In reaction to that, and especially disillusioned by the integration of the International Missionary Council into the World Council of Churches, evangelically-minded folks in Europe and North America stressed verbal proclamation that would seek personal conversion to Jesus Christ over-against socio-political agendas. The Civil Rights movement in the U.S. and liberation theology movements in Latin America, the Philippines, South Korea, India and elsewhere exacerbated the split.

When Church and Mission are confused and fused, and when mission is made to stand for any and all activities that the church may want to carry out in the world, then Stephen Neill's dictum seems to prove true: "When everything is mission, nothing is mission" (1959:81).

I do not believe anyone was really satisfied with the dichotomy between social action and verbal evangelism. The 1970s and 1980s involved multiple attempts to narrow the gap. The Lausanne Movement birthed a number of consultations, papers, and gatherings seeking to re-think the matter of the "priority of evangelism" as it had been articulated in the Lausanne Covenant. In the 1970s Arthur Glasser sought to develop the notion of the Kingdom of God as a way of bringing evangelism and social action closer together. Today, there is a very substantial global consensus around the Kingdom of God theme as a way of building a more holistic view of mission. This motif has been prominent in the theology of mission of Rene Padilla and his associates in the Latin American Theological Fraternity. Drawing from the Kingdom of God theme, they have developed the idea of "integral mission" as a conceptual framework that might bridge the gap between verbal proclamation and social action.

Thus, in the 1980s and 1990s we see evangelical perspectives of mission beginning to be interested in a "holistic" approach to mission. I believe an impetus for this may be the second- and third-generation converts and maturing churches in Africa, Asia, and Latin America. These converts, fruit of the early evangelization of these Western evangelical mission societies, have begun to search for ways in which the Gospel they accepted may impact the socio-economic, cultural and political realities in which they find themselves. These new generations of converts are now living in circumstances of oppression, persecution, disease, hunger, and abject poverty. And they are beginning to ask their brothers and sisters in the West what the impact of the Gospel upon the reality they are now experiencing should be.

With the decline of the church in the West, and the center of gravity shifting so that two-thirds of all world Christianity is now in Asia, Africa, Latin America and Oceania, the Church of Jesus is increasingly a church of the poor and oppressed. One might say that for the first time since Constantine, over 1600 years ago, the world church has the potential of constructing its understanding of mission with the building blocks drawn from the experience, life, vitality, and vision of churches and missions in the south and east of the globe, as well as the north and the west. All this leads to a desire to re-think and re-conceptualize the nature of mission at the beginning of this new century.

## The Present Situation: Recovering Believability

With two-thirds of world Christianity located now in the South and East, I believe that one of the most significant issues of global/local mission on, from, and to six continents in today's world will involve the believability of the Church and its mission. From the perspective of those who are not yet Christians, amidst the marketplace of competing religious affiliations in a global climate of profound spiritual hunger and curiosity, is the Church and its mission believable? It would appear that earlier attempts to articulate a relevant theology of mission have fallen short.

In Romans 12:2, the Apostle Paul admonishes his hearers, "Do not be conformed to this world, but be transformed by the renewing of your minds, so that you may discern what is the will of God — what is good and acceptable and perfect." Paul here calls for metamorphosis! A missiology of metamorphosis would entail the kind of mission that we see in the transformation of the woman of Sychar — and of the village of Sychar — in John 4. Metamorphosis is the word used to describe the phenomenal transformation that happens when a chrysalis becomes a butterfly. I believe a biblical missiology of transformation envisions just such a change in

Our resource centre in Springvale, Australia, was bursting at the seams. As we tried to find a new centre, we did not know that the circumstances of God's provision would echo those of the sixth-century founder of Western monasticism, Benedict of Nursia.

It was the Friday before Christmas 2000. Rain poured down as I made my way home from the old shopfront that had been our centre for the past seven years. As I began to scamper home, I passed a real estate agent's office. Our previous attempts at finding a new centre had failed, and that morning when I looked in the office window I sensed God saying, "Trust me."

"It beats getting wet," I thought. After explaining yet again to Edvard, the Ukrainian real estate agent, that we wanted a place for training, worship, meetings, and administration, he suddenly started beaming.

"You don't need a shopfront. You need a Buddhist temple!"

After driving through the torrential rain to pick up the key, we found the weatherboard house in Springvale that had been converted into a temple. There were colored lights, a Buddhist statue in the front garden and signs saying, "Sri Lankan Buddhist Society of Victoria." I understood that this place was a monastery for monks and a temple for the Sri Lankan community—a fact grasped more profoundly when we walked through the front door into that sweet, musty smell of incense.

As we entered the green kitchen, we looked out on the covered, brick-paved backyard, and I could picture the prayer, hospitality, and planning that this place could help generate for mission. "We shape buildings or our buildings shape us," was the way we had conducted a recent review meeting. We did not want a mission compound so much as a place to refresh and equip workers and communities facing poverty in Australia and beyond.

I rambled on about the temple. "It does have the space we need, that's for sure. It would change the type of centre we have, though. It wouldn't be a walk-off-the-street welfare centre, but a resourcing centre. It isn't as close to the train station but it is closer to Social Security. Wonder what the rest of the team and supporters will think of us taking over a Buddhist temple? Is this the place God has been preparing for us all along?" Remembering that Benedict began his enduring ministry on the site of a temple to Apollo, we decided to move forward.

 Although it was the time of year when "nothing much gets done in Australia," it took less than two weeks and a whirl of prayer, phone calls, emails, and meetings for us to have a deposit paid. The asking price of $185,000 came down to $168,000. In a space of days, $94,000 came together. We then invited people to help "redeem" the centre for Christian mission with us.

I try not to smile too much when explaining to Christians that we bought a Buddhist temple. I expected reactions. But we have had nothing but positive comments. In the face of so many old churches being turned into apartments, redeeming a Buddhist temple seemed right.

The way God provides is amazing. As often happens, it is when we are at a total loss that something comes through. I shudder to think of some of the other properties Edvard showed us. I am not sure why prayers are not always answered quickly, but I do know that the waiting provides an opening for God's way to be detected and followed. Redeeming a former Buddhist temple is a symbolic action that ushered in a new phase in our history as a gospel community. Even St. Benedict played his part.

**Ashley, serving in Thailand**

persons, social structures and nations of our world because of the Gospel of the Kingdom and the work of the Holy Spirit.

Such a missiology of metamorphosis would involve the kind of radical change we see in Paul after meeting Jesus on the Damascus road. This is God's mission that "rescued us from the power of darkness and transferred us into the kingdom of his beloved Son, in whom we have redemption, the forgiveness of sins" (Colossians 1:13-14). This is such a profound, all-pervasive transformation that Paul would end up saying, "I have been crucified with Christ; and it is no longer I who live, but it is Christ who lives in me. And the life I now live in the flesh I live by faith in the Son of God, who loved me and gave himself for me" (Galatians 2:19-20).

This is a missiology that seeks to turn the world upside down. Because the Church's mission is to participate in Jesus' mission — and Jesus' mission sets the parameters of the Church's mission — the Christian Church-in-mission intends to "bring good news to the poor ... to proclaim release to the captives and recovery of sight to the blind, to let the oppressed go free, to proclaim the year of the Lord's favor" (Luke 4:18-19).

# Recreation in a Century: Seeking a Missiology of Transformation

How, then, may we go about constructing a Trinitarian, Kingdom-based Missiology of Transformation? It seems to me that a first step would be to affirm that mission is not fundamentally ours: it does not belong to the church, it is not the property of mission agencies, it is not owned by the Christian NGO's (non-governmental organizations). It is not for us to determine the content or parameters of our mission. Rather, mission is most fundamentally God's mission: it is *missio Dei*. This being true, it is essential that we construct a theological foundation on which to build the rest of the superstructure of a Missiology of Transformation. Such a foundation cannot be essentially anthropological or strategic, demographic or linguistic, political or economic, sociological, psychological, or political. It is also not determined by the needs, demands or aspirations of our target audiences. The pilings driven into the soft earth of our various contexts, pilings that will support the structure of missiology of transformation, must be theological truths drawn from Scripture and from the Church's understanding of God learned throughout twenty centuries of the Church's experience and reflection of God.

In order to make this idea more concrete, I want to describe in broad strokes, in the form of a set of summary statements, what I believe could be the content of a Trinitarian, Kingdom-based Missiology of Transformation. We begin, then, as does the Bible with affirmations about God the Father Almighty, creator of heaven and earth.

## God the Father

Christians care for creation not because it is "mother earth" (New Age paganism), nor because its care guarantees the survival of the human race (secular humanism), but rather because it is the creation of, and is cared for and supported by our heavenly Father in Jesus Christ (Psalm 8, John 1, Colossians 1, and Ephesians 1). We know that there is a link between the salvation of humans and the salvation of the earth. For "the creation waits with eager longing for the revealing of the children of God. ... in hope that the creation itself will be set free from its bondage to decay and will obtain the freedom of the glory of the children of God" (Romans 8:19-22). And we know that the status of creation is intimately connected with the relationship of humans with God. When humans rebelled against God in the Garden of Eden, creation itself fell. And now "we know that the whole creation has been groaning in labor pains until now ... (because) the creation waits with eager longing for the revealing of the children of God" (Romans 8:22,19). God is always, at all times, actively involved in the preservation and re-creation of all that is. Thus a Missiology of Transformation that participates in the mission Dei involves Christians in the care, preservation, and re-creation of all the created order.

All humans are members of the same human family created by the same God (Genesis 1-3, John 1). And all human life is intrinsically valuable because, though fallen, it is created by God, in God's image. Thus, as children of the Creator God, Christians are inherently against all that dehumanizes and destroys life. A Missiology of Transformation will involve a profound commitment to affirming all that values, cares for, and enhances human life. The God of the Bible loves all humans equally. "For God so loved the world" (John 3:16) includes all humanity, including all those who are not yet Christian. So, a Missiology of Transformation will seek by all legitimate means to call all peoples to a living faith relationship with their Creator in Jesus Christ by grace through faith granted us by the Holy Spirit.

Because God the Creator of all has placed humans as stewards over God's creation, a missiology of transformation is a missiology of stewardship. This stewardship is not merely the careful and wise use of what you and I have. Rather, it is the careful, purposeful and loving care of all that belongs to God. And all that we have belongs to God. Christians understand that it is their God-given responsibility and calling to be stewards of all that God has created (Genesis 1-3, Psalm 8, Hebrews 2:6-9).

The God of the Bible is a compassionate God, slow to anger and abounding in mercy who would not have any perish but desires that everyone should come to repentance (2 Peter 3:9). Thus we as Christians love all other human beings because God first loved them and gave his life for them—in that while we all were yet sinners, Christ died for us and for them (Romans 5:8) Our motivation for mission derives from God's creation,

God's love, God's mission, and God's desire. To be "children of God" (John 1:12) entails participating in God's mission. We are, therefore eager to preach the gospel to all peoples because we are in fact debtors "both to Greeks and to barbarians, both to the wise and to the foolish" (Romans 1:14). We participate in our Father's calling all people to Himself, for "no one who believes in him will be put to shame. For there is no distinction between Jew and Greek; the same Lord is Lord of all and is generous to all who call on him. For 'Everyone who calls on the name of the Lord shall be saved'" (Romans 10:11-13).

## God the Son: Jesus the Christ

Christians in conversation with people of other faiths confess there is salvation in no one else: only through faith in Jesus Christ (Acts 4:12). A Missiology of Transformation will acknowledge the general revelation that God has shone in the midst of other faiths, but will affirm as well that only in Jesus Christ is God's revelation complete — and only in Jesus Christ is there salvation.

The Incarnation shows us that salvation involves the creation of a completely new person, for "if anyone is in Christ, there is a new creation: everything old has passed away; see, everything has become new!" (2 Corinthians 5:17). Thus a Missiology of Transformation will be involved in the creation and re-creation of persons, seeking for them to become fully complete, fully human in Jesus Christ.

Incarnational contextuality points us to receptor-oriented communication and contextualization. Jesus adapted His mission not only to humans, but also to specific humans: e.g., compare His mission with Nicodemus to His mission with the woman of Sychar (John 3 and 4).

The content of the Church's mission is defined and circumscribed by Jesus' mission. In Luke 4, Jesus describes and declares the essence of His mission. Drawing from the way the New

Testament describes Jesus' messianic mission, as the Body of Christ, the Church's mission involves at least *koinonia*, *kerygma*, *diakonia*, and *marturia* by being for the world a community of Prophets, Priests, Kings, Healers, Liberators and Sages as the loving Community of the King.

A christological foundation of a Missiology of Transformation will involve discipleship in two senses. First, our Great Commission calling is to make disciples; to call, invite, and gather those who will become disciples of Jesus Christ. Secondly, Christ's disciples are to present their bodies as living sacrifices with a view to being continually transformed in order to "discern what is the will of God — what is good and acceptable and perfect" (Romans 12:2). As disciples of Jesus we are by nature missionary disciples and Christ's love compels us to be ambassadors of reconciliation in a hurting, troubled and conflicted world (2 Corinthians 5:11-21).

Christ's lordship is lordship over all humans. One day, every knee will bow to His lordship (Philippians 2). Our privilege, right, and duty are to proclaim the Gospel of the Kingdom that Jesus is Lord in every corner of the globe, among every people group, to every person. Christ's lordship is also over the principalities and powers of this world, including global economic, political, social, and structural centers of power.

### God the Holy Spirit

The Holy Spirit transforms all of life — every aspect and all facets of one's life. Thus, a pneumatologically-grounded Missiology of Transformation will seek the creation and re-creation of the whole person, permeating all relationships and human structures relative to that person's life.

The Holy Spirit convicts the world of guilt in regard to sin and righteousness and judgment (John 16:8). The Holy Spirit transforms persons, giving them grace and faith to believe in

Jesus Christ. The Holy Spirit is the agent of transformation of persons from inside out. Conversion is not possible except by the work of the Holy Spirit. Thus a Missiology of Transformation can only happen through the work of the Holy Spirit. A missiology of transformation will seek, in the power of the Holy Spirit, to create and re-create the spiritual life of persons along with the physical, social, emotional and intellectual aspects of their being. A corollary of this is to recognize that a pneumatological Missiology of Transformation will by its very nature involve a variety of forms of spiritual warfare.

A pneumatologically-grounded Missiology of Transformation entails the realization that only the Holy Spirit creates the Church -- and only the Holy Spirit empowers and directs the Church's mission. The Holy Spirit forms, transforms and re-forms the Church to be, know, do, serve, and relate in ways depicted by a host of biblical metaphors of the Church-in-mission, such as salt of the earth, light of the world, earthen vessels filled with the pearls of the Gospel, Body of Christ, a new humanity, ambassadors of reconciliation, the Family of God, among many others. The spirituality of Christians, of churches, and of mission agencies must be transformed through the ministry of the Holy Spirit and directed in mission to a lost and hurting world so loved by God.

The gifts of the Holy Spirit are given to the Church for mission in the world. And the fruits of the Holy Spirit are the Spirit's gift to the world through the presence of the community of faith that embodies that fruit. Our world is in desperate need of the fruit of the Holy Spirit: love, joy, peace, patience, kindness goodness, faithfulness, gentleness, and self-control (Galatians 5:22). And this fruit is based on people living out the Decalogue in love of God and neighbor. Such fruit, in the power of the Holy Spirit will radically transform -- it will fundamentally alter the realities in which we live today.

Jesus Christ rules in the Kingdom through the ministry of the Holy Spirit. We cannot have a kingdom missiology unless we have an equally broad, deep, high, and wide pneumatological conception and praxis in mission.

As the down payment of eternal life (Ephesians 1:14), the Holy Spirit creates hope for the coming of the Kingdom in Jesus Christ. A pneumatologically-grounded Missiology of Transformation will eagerly await the final day when Christ returns and the final, full transformation will occur in a new heaven and a new earth. Then transformed Christians in a transformed reality will gather around the throne of the Lamb and sing, "Worthy is the Lamb that was slaughtered to receive power and wealth and wisdom and might and honor and glory and blessing!" (Revelation 5:12).

The summary statements offered above are but an outline of what I believe is involved in articulating the theological underpinnings of a missiology of transformation. At the heart of this vision is a commitment to radical change.

# Conclusion

Global/local mission in the twenty-first century must be contextually and culturally appropriate to the needs, aspirations, worldviews, and agenda of the persons in each context. In order to meet such demands, a Missiology of Transformation will need to be based on a Trinitarian view of mission that is in continuity with what we have learned about mission during the past one hundred years and also in rather significant discontinuity with mission praxis as that seems to be the essence of the concept of transformation A missiology of transformation involves *Trans* and *Formation*, discontinuity and change coupled with continuity and re-creation.

# Trans (discontinuity)

A missiology of transformation calls for movement, for metamorphosis, for change, for conversion, for a change of heart. Without a change of heart, a change of self, of being, nothing will change. Merely a change of religious affiliation, merely an individual, vertical conversion will not change the persons, structures, systems and cultures of this world. To be believable, the Church and Christians must be good for something – they must be able to demonstrate to the people of their contexts and nations that they have something concrete, measurable, visible, positive, constructive and helpful to offer their contexts and nations. This calls for radical conversion as much of the Church and of Christians to their mission of being Christ's transforming presence in the world – just as much as conversion of non-Christians to faith in Jesus Christ.

# Formation (continuity)

A Missiology of Transformation also calls for incarnational contextuality, for wrestling with the relationship of Gospel and culture in thousands of different contexts worldwide. This transformation is not merely a change of religious affiliation, not merely a matter of new church membership. This is not merely civilization or education, or a change of ethical behavior; it is not merely socio-economic and political betterment. Rather, a Missiology of Transformation entails the new formation, the re-creation of whole persons — of all and every aspect of their lives, each in their particular context in terms of knowing, being, doing, serving, and relating to one another: It has simultaneously personal, social, structural and national implications. It involves reconciliation with God, self, creation, others, and the socio-cultural structures.

John ends his gospel by saying, "Now Jesus did many other signs in the presence of his disciples, which are not written in this book. But these are written so that you may come to believe ... [that] you may have life in his name" (John 20:30-31). Like a sponge is permeated with water, so our mission is to offer new life to the women and men of our world of the twenty-first century in which all of their life, every aspect of life, all arenas of life are permeated with the presence of God the Father, Son, and Holy Spirit. The rich and powerful of this world need to be transformed, they need to be converted, just as much as the poor and the weak.

This is a time of massive social change in Africa, Asia, Eastern Europe, and Latin America — as well as the cities of Western Europe, Australia, and North America. The Church of Jesus Christ is there to proclaim the Gospel and contribute to the building of new nations and the rebuilding of old ones. The Church of Jesus Christ stands for love, joy, peace, reconciliation and the value of human life.

## Reference Cited

Neill, Stephen
    1959    *Creative Tension*. London: Edinburgh House Press.

# 7

# HIV/AIDS: Avenues of Involvement for the Church

by Doug Priest

## An Attitude of Humility through Repentance

The church, particularly the church in the West, has been slow to become involved in the HIV/AIDS pandemic. Seemingly forgetting that Christ lived a life of compassion and did not question the source of a person's illness, many in the church have seen AIDS as God's judgment being rained down upon those who engage in the sins of homosexuality, intravenous drug use, and prostitution. While showing some sympathy for those affected by tainted blood transfusion and transmission from mother to unborn child, the church has been slow to acknowledge that in the majority of the world's HIV/AIDS comes from heterosexual activity, the same sort of activity that is daily promoted around the world by the Western media and entertainment industry.

Since the number of those with HIV/AIDS is highest in Africa and Asia, Westerners have for too long turned a blind eye to their suffering. Even in the West, those suffering from AIDS have been stigmatized and forgotten by the church. Many have faced death alone and uncomforted.

Many Christians, because of their belief that the advocacy of condom use encourages a higher rate of premarital sex, have refused to acknowledge that condoms, when used correctly and consistently, are 90 percent effective against the spread of HIV/AIDS.

HIV/AIDS is no respecter of persons. Believers and unbelievers alike are affected. Research has indicated that, tragically, evangelical Christians are some of the least likely to become involved in the battle against AIDS or to contribute to the needs of those orphaned by AIDS.

The church today must repent and seek forgiveness from God for our sins of apathy, indifference, despair, condemnation, and lack of compassion for those suffering from this horrible disease.

## An Attitude of Service through Compassion

We of the household of faith must in loving service join hands with those who are suffering. Like believers confronting those suffering from the Black Death during the Middle Ages, we must run to the sick rather than from them.

The church has a worldwide reach. Situated close to 90 percent of the world's poor, it can easily connect with the grassroots. Ten million children a year die from diseases such as pneumonia, diarrhea, and malaria, each of which is preventable for a few cents a day for each child. Many of these children are infected with HIV. Bringing resources to these problems—as well as health issues such as sexually transmitted diseases, nutrition, and clean water—will result in significant life extension. A longer life will provide time to get more data about anti-retroviral (ARV) drugs, to develop the infrastructure so that ARV medication is affordable and available, and to develop a cure. Since faith-based organizations carry out more than 50 percent of the health care in many African countries, the

Staring into the face of a man that can hardly be described as a man, I tried to concentrate on the task at hand. The smells and oppressive heat made me feel weak. But my task was to massage and to apply various creams and ointments on the bodies of the 38 patients that lay there every day waiting to die of AIDS-related illnesses.

As soon as someone died the bed would be filled by another emaciated, scab-covered soul who would join this queue of death. AIDS is called the curse of Thailand (and many other countries, I am sure). Some northern villages see as many as five people die every day. In Klong Toey, the slum where we stayed, the lucky ones got these beds.

I was a volunteer with the Human Development Centre in Klong Toey, Bangkok's largest slum. The slum house where we stayed was a scene of many adventures, such as the regular floods, rats and cockroaches, as well as the traffic of people in strange and bizarre states after buying their drugs from people in the apartment upstairs.

I had to come to terms with the death of the young men and women at the hospice. I would give a woman a massage one day and find her gone the next. I felt relief for those who died, as their pain had finally stopped, but sadness for all those that looked on. One man said he wished he had died, but that he was terrified of dying.

I struggled with the fact that my Thai language was so limited that I could not share Christ with anyone. Each day an Italian priest who spoke Thai and English would talk with and pray for each patient. A number of the patients told me that they had become Christians through this ministry.

Each day I looked forward to going to the hospice, and God taught me much through my experiences there. I realized I could not fix anything or make anybody better. The pain these patients were racked with was terrible, and I imagined each as Jesus, lying there and waiting for crucifixion.

**Anji, serving in Thailand**

church needs to show compassion by increasing giving to such organizations.

The Bible instructs us to care for widows and orphans. The HIV/AIDS crisis and its effects will be with us well into the future. Entire generations are being decimated, including teachers, health workers, public servants, and church leaders.

The number of AIDS orphans in different areas peaks approximately 10 years after the number of AIDS deaths has peaked.

When facing the growing number of AIDS orphans, the church must not make decisions based on guilt or a naïve belief that there are quick and easy solutions. Building orphanages to house and care for orphans should be an option only after all other alternatives have been considered. In addition to issues of social dislocation, research from Africa indicates that the annual cost to care for an orphan in an institution is $1,000—versus $150 for foster care.

Those suffering from AIDS need our compassion. We need to visit them, talk with them of our eternal hope, and embrace them in the name of Christ.

**An Attitude of Involvement through Ministry**

An African proverb says, "The best time to plant a tree is 20 years ago; the next best time is today." Though it is late, Christians must now take the lead in increasing public awareness about AIDS and AIDS prevention. We need educational efforts at all levels and through all means. After we become educated about HIV/AIDS, we can educate others. We need articles, bulletin inserts, letters to the editor, campaigns, stories, sermons, dramas, art, and public presentations. We should provide money for a wide variety of educational endeavors all over the world.

The HIV/AIDS disease spreads primarily by sexual behavior, which in turn emerges from personal and cultural values. The church can speak about values in ways that others cannot or will not. Two-thirds of those who become affected with HIV/AIDS are 15 to 24 years old. Instruction about risk reduction must begin at an early age. Almost one-third of the world's population is 15 years or younger. The vast majority of them are AIDS-free. Along with the church, parents must be equipped to teach their children about AIDS. Children, the abstinent, and those who remain faithful to their marriage partners do not need messages about condoms. However, those involved with multiple-partners do.

The church must mobilize. Almost all local congregations in the West have members in medical fields. They can teach, share experiences, and go on short-term medical trips. A Western church can partner with a church or a community from Africa, Asia, or the former Soviet Union and share resources to help its partner address AIDS in an appropriate manner.

A cell-church of 8,000 members in Kampala, Uganda, determined that each of its cell groups would care for one orphan or for one family whose head of household had died due to AIDS. Can we who have so much more do less?

# Action Steps

The crisis affords the church the opportunity to demonstrate Christ's concern for the suffering. How we respond will be the church's defining issue for the next 50 years. We should take the following five steps immediately:

- Encourage your church (local congregation and denomination) to commit a minimum of 1-3% of its resources annually—people, pulpit time, and finances—to HIV/AIDS awareness and involvement.

- Encourage your church (local congregation and denomination) to empower an AIDS task force to research and educate, then allocate these congregational resources.
- Advocate, either directly or through appropriate agencies, that regional and national government bodies set aside additional resources to address HIV/AIDS.
- Uphold through prayer those who are suffering from HIV/AIDS and those who are involved at all levels in addressing and combating HIV/AIDS.
- Boldly promote the A-B-C strategy: A = Abstinence from sexual intercourse until marriage; B = Being faithful to one partner; and (when A and B are not being followed), C = Correct and consistent use of condoms.

As we serve with the Maasai churches of Christ in Kenya, we are finding many ways to address the AIDS epidemic there.

### AIDS Education

Within the last two years the clinic system and the local churches have begun a cooperative program of providing three- to five-day AIDS seminars at the village level. The goals of these seminars are: (1) to emphasize biblical principles of sexual purity as the means to prevent AIDS transmission and block the wave of the AIDS epidemic; and (2) to encourage the church to care for AIDS victims and orphans. The churches host the seminars while clinical medical workers, church leaders, or guests provide the lessons.

The Narok town church has formed an AIDS drama troupe consisting of church members who write and perform plays depicting the causes and consequences of AIDS. The dramas, which are usually followed by a sermon or an object lesson, are performed in area churches. The troupe won a prize at a national competition for AIDS dramas. We hope that the troupe will also be able to perform in village seminars in the future. We are thankful to U.S. churches who support this ministry.

### AIDS Testing and Counseling

The laboratory at the Ewaso Ng'iro clinic provides HIV testing as well as pre- and post-test counseling. A Peace Corps volunteer conducts an introductory counseling session in a private room prior to the blood test for any patient a nurse suspects might have the virus. Patients with positive results are counseled again, with instruction to: (1) visit the Voluntary Counseling and Testing Center in Narok town for a second confirmatory test; (2) bring any other sexual partners in for testing; and (3) adhere to biblical principles of abstinence before marriage and faithfulness in marriage to avoid transmitting the virus to others.

### Care for AIDS Patients

All of our clinics are directly affected by the AIDS epidemic. Whereas we saw only 10 to 12 cases of AIDS during our first six years in Kenya, we now see three to four new cases of AIDS each time we visit the clinic at Ewaso Ng'iro. The clinic records two new positive tests per day.

We care for several hundred AIDS patients on a regular basis. Those who test positive for HIV are encouraged to enroll in the program in which they receive prophylactic medications (to prevent PCP pneumonia and fungal infections), vitamins and nutritional supplements each month. As patients demonstrate compliance in the program, antiretroviral (ARV) medications are added as necessitated by disease stage. The patients are followed closely by community health workers who visit them in their homes to provide moral and spiritual support. This program has dramatically improved the health and extended the lives of many with HIV/AIDS.

### Future Plans

We hope soon to have trained and registered AIDS counselors to help us expand our program. We will likely have the Neviraprine medical program which tests pregnant women and provides medication at the time of delivery for the mother and newborn. This program decreases transmission of the AIDS virus by 30 percent.

We will also probably begin an active ARV therapy program, which will provide medicine to contain the illness as well as provide regular follow-up and counseling to the patients. The ARV medications are still prohibitively expensive for the average Maasai patient, but would be within the means of some. We hope that cheaper medications will become available in the future. However, the truest and best way to reverse the epidemic is through prevention, so the education mentioned above, spearheaded by the church, is our primary goal.

**David and Susan, serving in Kenya**

# 8

# Changing a Community

by Florence Muindi

It was a wet day. Driving through the Mekanisa slums in Addis Ababa, Ethiopia, towards our house beyond this community, I spotted my friend Tadesse. Tadesse was a young man who had been requesting that my family and I visit his church in the slums. Waving me to stop, he made the invitation again, which I agreed to. He joined us in the car to go to his church. We took a narrow detour, with the deep potholes challenging the Toyota pickup. On both sides of this drive were plastic and mud houses, measuring on average ten by ten feet. Poorly dressed and dirty children with no shoes ran back and forth across the street. Some stood by their houses, while others played with the pools of water by the road left by a recent rainfall. Uncollected waste littered the community.

Arriving at the rented house which was the community church, I immediately regretted that I had agreed to come. It was muddy. I knew the black cotton soil would cake around our shoes and I hesitated to step out of the car. It was, however, too late to turn back.

Once inside the church, we were given a short history as we stood near a poorly constructed pulpit. They had started meeting two years ago, initially as a fellowship, in a missions compound. When the mission closed, the church moved out to this house. The church was hosting a compassion project, sponsoring 320 children from the surrounding homes. About twenty-five members gathered each Sunday morning to worship.

As we concluded the discussion in prayer and I was getting ready to leave, I heard a voice behind me say, "You will come back to this church and preach the word from this pulpit." I turned around, thinking of it as a big joke from my friend Tadesse, but there was no one there! Then panic came, as I realized God was calling me to minister in this church! Well, that would take a lot of courage, the absence of rain and would certainly be a long time down the line. Or so I thought, since I was only halfway through my language school.

Every time we drove through this community, the misery and evident needs burdened me. I decided to start from a safe place, to invite the children to our home and do a Vacation Bible School (VBS) over the Easter break. I put a poster on our gate, announcing the VBS, and calling on those interested to come the next morning for registration. I shouldn't have said morning!

We woke up at 6 a.m. to a deafening noise from the gate the next day. All the children from the slum had come to register for the VBS. We registered a maximum of 400 and sent the rest away. About the same number stayed outside our gate all day, hoping we would take them in.

There was no way I could manage a VBS of this number, so I went back to the community church in a hurry, needing help. I recruited ten teachers and we survived the VBS. On the last day, in a worship and prayer session with the participating teachers, we committed to begin a regular Bible study. This led to another Bible study and by the summer, I was leading four Bible studies a week, targeting the slum community.

Next came another request from the church pastor. He asked me if, as a medical doctor, I could do a health screening for the 320 children their compassion project was targeting. How could I say no?

With the help of a missionary doctor, a colleague, we did medical examinations on the children over three days. Then, it happened. The ugliness of the situation was revealed. How could I see this and walk away?

85% of the 320 children seen had an active disease process. The five top diseases were worm infestation, skin diseases, eye infections, respiratory infections and AIDS related illnesses. 60% had more than one disease process. Although they all walked away with medicines for these illnesses, close to 100% of them would revert to the same status within three months after treatment when subjected to the existing living conditions. No, curative care was not the solution. It would be like attempting to dry the floor flooding from a leaking roof. We had to fix the roof.

Years before, God had called me to a three-fold ministry to the poor: heal, feed and deliver. Heal their diseases through health education, treatment and primary health care interventions. Feed the hungry through nutrition education, food provision, income generation, micro entrepreneurships and skills training. Deliver from the cycle of poverty, break the yoke of Satan, the slavery to sin so that they may have life and have it in abundance.

The ministry began. The local church had to be the agent of change, and they agreed to this challenge. A holistic approach to change the status of the community was agreed on. They chose eight people for me to train on how to implement this change. These eight people became the very first training team. After a ten day training based on a self-developed curriculum from training materials used by the African Medical and Research

# Wildfire:
## An HIV/AIDS Awareness Group Exercise

**Note for the Facilitator:** Wildfire is a very powerful sensitizing activity that needs to be guided by a skilled and experienced facilitator. Some participants may feel varying degrees of distress at being put in the role of an HIV positive person.

It is essential to alert participants from the beginning that the exercise is designed to give them an opportunity to experience what it might feel like to discover that one has been exposed to the virus. This is a simulation for learning purposes and in no way implies or suggests anything about peoples' real lives and HIV status. To permit the discussion of sensitive issues with complete trust, observers are not allowed. Participation by all should be encouraged, not only because of what individuals learn from the activity but also because of how powerful the activity can be in helping to build a sense of intimacy and purpose within the group. Those who do not wish to participate in the exercise should be given the opportunity to leave the room.

**Purpose:** To help participants experience intimately the feelings and reactions of a person living with HIV/AIDS as well as those of others who are not infected. To create awareness of how quickly and covertly the virus spreads and the deep emotional rifts (and bonds) it can create between people.

**Time:** One hour is needed for the exercise.

**Materials:** Cards or small pieces of paper to be handed out to all participants at the time of getting test results, both for the initial test and for the re-test. Half of the cards should read "your test result is positive" and the other half should read "your test result is negative."

**Stage One:** Ask the participants to stand up and listen carefully to the instructions. Inform the participants that you will be moving around within the group and shaking hands of as many of them as possible. While doing this, you will lightly scratch the hand of ONLY ONE participant with your middle finger to indicate that he/she had been exposed to the virus. At this point insure that no one else can identify who that person is.

Withdraw yourself from the group but ask participants to continue shaking hands among themselves in a normal way. The person whose palm you have scratched should similarly scratch the palm of two other people.

**Stage Two:** When three rounds of handshaking have been completed, ask all the participants to form a circle. Then ask all those whose palms were scratched to come forward and form an inner circle. Explain that they have been exposed to the virus. Ask them to describe how they feel under these circumstances. Some examples of the responses might be: "nervous", "lost", or "scared".

Ask them what they would like to do at this point. Suggest to them the possibility of going for a test. What do they need to take into consideration before having the test? Who would they tell the result to and how might they react? How would it feel to be negative? Positive? Those who wish to be tested should then be handed a card that shows either a positive or a negative result.

Now address specifically those who have tested HIV positive. How do you feel about your test results? Responses may include: "alienated", "alone", "discriminated against", "extremely unlucky", "scared", "want to lead a healthy life", "there must be some mistake", "hope nobody gets to know of it".

Next address those whose test results were negative: "How do you feel about your status now?" They may give varied responses, "lucky", "guilty", "more willing to support people who are positive". When they have finished with their responses ask them to leave the inner circle and rejoin the outer circle. Those who have tested positive must remain where they are.

At this point you can open up a general discussion by asking questions such as:

When your hand was scratched and you shook hands with others, what was going through your mind knowing now that you might have been infecting someone?

Could the participants tell who was positive?

Did those whose results were negative trust the results? How many wanted to be re-tested?

**Conclusion:** In this exercise the participants who test "positive" may feel uncomfortable. It is important for the facilitator to be sensitive to this and to insure not only that they come out of role but that they receive any support they need to disengage from the exercise.

Foundation (AMREF) as well as a resource book written by Stan Rowland on Community Health Evangelism (CHE), we were equipped to start.

Following the training team graduation and after a time of prayer and fasting, the first activity was to invite the community members, especially those with children seen in our first health screening, to come to the church to discuss the findings of the health screening. They came in hundreds and gathered in the church. It was the work of the trained team members to discuss what had been found and the causes. I stayed home to pray. They were to bring up the fact that medicine was not the solution. The community was responsible to ensure health for all. They ended with a charged and committed community wanting to see change. They chose nine committee members to plan for this change, half of whom ended up being church members!

The next activity was to train this committee on issues of development, health, community organizing and transformation strategies. They were convinced they had the answer. On graduating, they were to call the community together to choose health promoters, one for every ten households. The church also chose health promoters, to pair up with those chosen by the community, so as to evangelize during home visits.

We organized the target community into nine clusters based on the geographical distribution of the 320 families we were targeting. These clusters would meet once every two weeks in the church to watch and discuss a clip of the Jesus film, as well as plan on health and development initiatives. These meetings were led by a committee member working with a training team member. A cluster had 30-40 families with a health promoter for every ten families. They took to cleaning public toilets, clearing drainages, repairing houses of the lepers among them and heaping and burning trash. All of these actions were community- based. The health promoters started home visits.

Prayer and health education were brought to the homes. We began to see the effects of our efforts in people's behavior.

Then we carried out a household survey to identify and prioritize needs. A very interesting factor came up. Some families in this community were fully dependent on begging as their only source of income. That led us to seek a grant from a church aid agency to begin a revolving fund project for micro entrepreneurship.

After a year of community mobilizing and organizing, we began interventions to bring about community transformation, in the physical and the spiritual sense. It was about this time that we noted the men were beginning to take a backseat, not wanting to participate and leaving intervention responsibilities to the women.

To address this, we planned a men-only dinner with a well-known speaker. We sent invitations to the men and they came. The sharing was centered on boosting their ego and highlighting their role. The speaker warned that if they did not take their position and own the community, their wives would take that role. They woke up, and have stayed awake.

Looking back after three years, some of the interventions implemented are:

- Vocational training in carpentry for men and tailoring for the women. Clusters are given chances to select candidates to benefit from these skills.
- Church-based kindergarten, teaching both children from the middle class who pay fees as well as from the very poor, who get free education and a midmorning snack.
- A micro enterprise program, benefiting several people in the community.
- A weekly women's ministry meeting.

The first time I met Aleg, I thought he was a new visitor. I was surprised to hear that he was a baptized believer, because my wife Heather and I hadn't seen him our first couple of months in Berdyansk. It wasn't until later that we heard his story. Aleg grew up in the church and was baptized, but later fell away and became an alcoholic. His wife Natasha was an alcoholic too. They had a son together, but several years later when Aleg turned back to the Lord, his wife divorced him.

For a couple of months, Aleg could be found at church every time the doors opened, but then he returned to his ex-wife and his old way of life. The church prayed for him, and once again he came back. At the end of one Sunday service, Aleg came to the front and prayed for forgiveness. The leaders of the congregation prayed with him.

About a month later, Aleg's ex-wife started coming to church. However, on Saturdays, we would see Natasha on the street, drunk and stumbling. She had to be about 30, but she looked 10, maybe 15, years older than that. I honestly wasn't sure it was such a good idea for her and Aleg to be going to the same church. They both needed help, and it seemed more likely that they would drag each other down than provide support for each other. A few weeks later, Natasha came forward at church and prayed for Jesus to come into her heart and be her Lord and Savior. A slow transformation began. During services one Sunday, Heather nudged me and said, "Do you recognize that woman over there?"

"No, should I?"

"It's Natasha," she replied. I couldn't believe my eyes. Natasha's expression, demeanor, clothes, hairstyle, even hair color (bleached blonde to God-given brown) had all changed. It was a pleasant surprise.

It is obvious that Aleg and Natasha love each other and want to be a family again. What can we do to help Aleg and Natasha and countless others in Berdyansk to stay clean and sober and get right with God? Our dream is to start a ministry devoted to them and their special needs.

**Jonathan, serving in Ukraine**

- A child sponsorship project, other than the original compassion project, meeting the needs of the poor children, initiated and organized by church members.
- A church based library and tutorial services to promote literacy.
- House and kitchen renovation efforts targeting the very poor, especially the lepers living in the community
- HIV/AIDS ministry with ten trained care and support providers. This ministry is headed by a nurse, who is a church member.

Inroads have been made into the community, and relationships have developed in a once violent situation. Rowdy gangs have come to the Lord. Short-term teams from the U.S. have come to work in the community alongside church members.

In the meantime, the church has grown to 350 members with 500 children participating weekly in the Sunday school program. Church members have grown spiritually with some of the church members, including Tadesse, taking seminary education. Worship has deepened. The prayer and intercession ministry is steady and powerful. Intercession is ongoing even during church services.

The most obvious change has been in the health indices. Health screening continued as a monitoring tool, initially every six months and later yearly. The percentage of the sick has steadily declined, despite the increase in HIV/AIDS, and has been a monitoring tool. It has declined from 85% to 74% to 59% and down to 53%. At this point we handed over the screening task to the church and they have continued to record improvement.

As per our phase out policy, this process of handing over leadership started in January 2003, and by the end of the year, our involvement will have ceased. We will leave behind a self-motivated, growing and empowered church, sustaining community interventions as well as a mobilized and organized community, participating and owning their health and developmental needs and advocating for change in a unified voice.

This community spread the news that together, change is possible. Before long, we were involved with two other communities basing interventions from local churches. This movement spread to other churches, urban and rural. We therefore sought help from Christian doctors, and registered a local non-governmental organization to own and replicate the piloted community transformation strategy. This has gone on to run tens of projects, in the region, across denominations. In the last two years, we have piloted holistic strategies to meet the needs of street children as well as individuals with HIV/AIDS.

This ministry now runs under a country board with an overseeing international board. The work is reaching out to several countries in the Horn and East African regions. It has been incorporated in the U.S. as a nonprofit organization, partnering with several agencies to declare the glory of God to the nations.

The financial challenge still remains, with the needs and desire for more interventions being more than can be met. Spiritual warfare has also been a major challenge, making us practically realize that the kingdom of God suffers violence and has to be taken by force. It has also woken us up to the need to pray. Traditionally, Mondays have become our days of prayer and fasting. On Tuesday evening, we meet with the training team representatives to pray for specific project needs and bring praises to the throne. We continue to press on, that we may achieve that which he has taken hold of us for. In each intervention and project we:

- look for appropriate interventions
- maximize local resources
- highlight participation -- community mobilization is a major activity
- address priority felt needs, honoring the choice made by the community—only sustainable interventions are implemented
- emphasize care for the whole person
- promote discernment and intercessory prayer
- proclaim the gospel, exalting this function of the church
- foster behavior change through education and example setting
- stress that poverty alleviation is integral to health
- guide the growth of the work through innovation, piloting, modeling and advocacy
- seek partnerships with suitable organizations
- follow the Jesus Model of Ministry, integrating physical and spiritual interventions

We continue to grow, learn, and adjust to new ways of being obedient to our Lord. We understand that change is necessary. It needs to be frequent; sometimes radical change is a necessity. We have to remain flexible.

We know that stopping to reconsider is important. Strategies, roles, frontiers, paradigms, partnership -- all must be subject to frequent evaluation.

God has an agenda for this generation which is different from that of the former generation. A wave is on to achieve this. It is wise to seek this wave and to ride on it.

It all began in the Spring of 2003 with a simple idea, a growing concern that our church needed to be a better neighbor to its community. Like most churches, the people of LifeSpring in Cincinnati had a desire to help people, meet needs, and serve meaningfully. We wanted to make a real difference in the lives of people, impacting not just our own members, but the community as a whole. Despite our commitments to overseas missions and inner city ministry, we realized that the average person who drove by our building every day probably knew very little about us, and likely did not see our church as an asset to the community. We believed that God was calling our church to meaningful ministry right in our own backyard. In the end, this simple idea mobilized 450 people and 5000 man hours of volunteer labor.

We began with the desire to demonstrate God's love in a very helpful, practical way. The challenge lay in finding a project that was big enough to challenge and inspire, yet was realistically attainable. We committed ourselves to take a fresh look at our community, not simply with a critical eye, but with a heart to help and improve the lives of our neighbors. We met with civic leaders, parachurch organizations, and other community leaders to discuss their vision for our community, and how we might support their efforts. It soon became clear that a project helping our local school district improve their facilities would be a perfect fit, and we committed to renovate the aging middle school building. "Deck The Halls" was born.

The project name was chosen to reflect the idea that this was our Christmas gift to the community. We would "deck" not only the hallways on all three floors, but also the lockers, 14 classrooms, a gym, cafeteria, and restrooms.

In September 2003, a leadership team began to meet regularly to lay out plans. None of us had any real experience with a project like this. But we divided the job into manageable pieces and people went to work on color and design, supplies, publicity, food (of course there was food!) and recruitment. We could only guess how long it might take to complete the renovations, but our time restrictions were short and non-negotiable. The project had to be completed during the 14 day Christmas break. Our costs estimates were also rough. We had set aside $10,000 for the project, and hoped that would be enough to do all of the work that needed to be done.

Fortunately, God knew exactly what was needed to get the job done: 450 workers contributing nearly 5000 hours, $6000 ($4000 under budget!), lots of donated materials, a professional architect, and dozens of key leaders working tirelessly to complete the project with excellence. We even finished up a day early and had an open house on the last day of the break.

The reaction from the community has been incredible. A contractor who loaned us scaffolding and other equipment was amazed that a church would tackle this type of project, and he was even more amazed to learn that we were on time and under budget. The reaction from the school has been overwhelming. The building principal couldn't believe the transformation. After the open house, she called to convey her gratitude by saying that while she was sure that there would be some improvement, she couldn't believe how far we had exceeded her expectations. Students were just as enthusiastic. They wrote thank you letters by the dozens, expressing how much they liked their school's new look. Teachers stopped by to share how much it improved their morale to know that the community cared about them.

The project also had an impact on our church. While it was fun to see the story on the news and in the papers, it's been even better to see how God has used "Deck the Halls" in the lives of people. We were overwhelmed by how many people in our church willingly gave up much of their Christmas holiday to serve. The Body of Christ was at work, each one using the gifts God gave. Many people who normally would not be "church leaders" stepped into major areas of servant leadership, and we saw God use them in amazing ways. It was great for so many people who don't fit the Sunday school teacher or choir member model to have the opportunity to use their gifts and talents to bring glory to God.

This was also one of the best intergenerational activities our church ever experienced. Children as young as 6 worked alongside men and women in their 70's. A lot of mutual respect, understanding, and affection grew as we sanded, scraped, washed down, and painted together. It was great to see entire families, from grandparents to little guys, leaving the school at the end of a shift talking about the fun they had working together. Even after the project was finished, these relationships have continued. People who didn't know each other before now share a special bond that comes from working alongside one another with the common goal of demonstrating Christ's love.

We recently celebrated the first baptism from "Deck the Halls." Our goal from the beginning was to plant seeds and open doors. We want to be a church that is recognized in our own neighborhood as a place where help and hope can be found. We pray that "Deck the Halls" is just the beginning of what God wants to do through us to reach our neighbors.

**Monica, serving in Cincinnati**

# 9

# Saved to Serve: Finding Motivation for Ministry

by Cory and Janice Lemke

We moved to the Crimean Peninsula of Ukraine, near the Black Sea, in 1995 and planned to work with the Evangelical Christian Baptist churches (ECB), an approximately 200-year-old denomination that suffered severe persecution under Soviet rule. The ECB churches tend to be legalistic, and some of their traditions differ from our own. Still, we agreed with their basic points of doctrine and thought we could work with them.

Our goal was to help develop leadership within the church, expand the church's vision, and help motivate its members for evangelism and church planting. Nevertheless, we entered Ukraine as learners, seeking to understand their background and situation. We tried to distinguish between cultural practices and biblical mandates. We wanted to pick our battles carefully, not simply strive to change everything that differed from American church practices. We believed God was at work in that culture, and His followers in Ukraine were ultimately responsible for reaching their own people with the Gospel.

In the summer and fall of 1997, Cory met with several local leaders within the ECB who wanted to reach people with the Gospel. They talked about how to rejuvenate the existing church and plant new ones. They shaped a strategy, discussed how to develop leaders and evangelists, and called the program the Efas Training Center.

"Efas" is the Russian equivalent of Ephesus. The name refers to the Apostle Paul's example in Acts 19:9-10 when he stayed in Ephesus and taught the disciples for two years. We assume he trained them in evangelism and church planting and sent them into the surrounding areas. The result: all who lived in Asia heard the word of the Lord.

In February of 1998, a two-year training course began for eleven men selected from Eastern Crimea as potential evangelists and church planters. Within two years, each of them had started at least one new church plant. In the summer of 2000, the Efas leadership team began training a second group, thirty-two men from all regions of Crimea. Most of these men also started at least one new church during their two-year training. A third group of twenty men began the two-year training course in 2004. This group was also successful in planting new churches.

We made mistakes and adjusted the program along the way. After the first group, we understood that we shouldn't take everyone who expressed an interest or each person church leaders recommended. We wanted men who were called and gifted for evangelism and church planting. We also wanted local churches to take ownership and participate in the church-planting process.

Even though most towns and villages lacked any church, most of the existing congregations had not yet overcome the reserved approach to ministry imposed on them during the Soviet system. A series of meetings with church leaders helped them understand the church-planting vision. These meetings focused on topics like God's heart for the lost and the purpose of the church. Efas leaders emphasized that they wanted to serve and strengthen the church, not simply take the most gifted men to meet our goals and leave the local church weak.

After laying this foundation of trust and understanding, the Efas leaders asked church leaders to recommend men they thought were gifted as evangelists and church planters. The potential students attended seminars over a period of four months, meeting once every three weeks for two days, usually Friday and Saturday. We got to know the men and observed if they had the gifts necessary to succeed in ministry. We listened to their testimonies, watched their interactions with others, saw if people came to Christ through their witness, and noted if they started a small group or church plant.

If they demonstrated that they had the skills and heart for this ministry, we invited them to participate in a more intensive, two-year training period. Lectures during the four-month seminar and the two-year training period focused primarily on three areas: vision (God loves everyone, not just Christians), the Gospel (what Jesus did for us), and practical aspects of ministry. Teachers encouraged the men to do more than simply form a new group of believers, but to disciple them, training them for ministry.

When the men talked about their impressions of the training center and things they thought were important, their comments most often fit into the first three categories: Fellowship, Gospel, and Practical Aspects of Ministry. When they talked about what motivated them, most responses pointed to the categories of Lordship or Call of God.

# Fellowship

Each of the church planters mentioned fellowship as an important aspect of the training. Besides the value of connection with other students, they talked about relationships with the leadership team, mentoring, modeling, and an atmosphere of trust and openness. Some of their quotes:

- We could compare notes…see how others were doing, what kinds of problems they were having, and how they resolved them. That kind of interaction was a big help. We would learn from each other.

- The fellowship and example that I had with the other men in the training really helped me. I was able to put things in context, and then things started coming together between the theory and practice.

- I saw other brothers who were involved in evangelistic ministry, and saw that I was not the only one who was burdened with reaching people with the Gospel. It was there that I saw how a team worked together. It helped motivate me, and they were an example for me. Now I try to encourage the groups I am working with to think and work and serve in terms of a team.

# Clarity of the Gospel

Having lacked Scripture during the Soviet era, the Ukrainian/ Russian church often focuses on legalism and tradition rather than on Jesus' words and message. To help overcome this, the training center emphasizes who Jesus is and what He accomplished by His incarnation, death, and resurrection.

Many church planters stressed that lessons on the Gospel were an important part of their training. When they understood God's grace, love, forgiveness, and mercy more clearly, they wanted to share that good news with others. They said:

- I remember we started with the question of 'What is the Gospel?' For me that was a revelation. I had been a believer for so many years, and had no idea what the Gospel was. That was a major turning point for me. I wanted to share what I learned with everyone. It was a very important part of my initial understanding of the Lord.

- I see that people are dying. Those who are forgiven much love much. I want others to see that Christ loves them, that God gives manna that fills us with everything that we need.
- I think that the biggest influence for me, and the most important thing of all was that so much time was spent on the Gospel. I came to understand the nuances of the Gospel myself, and when I gained clarity I was able to share it with others.
- We can read much, commentaries or other things, but the fact that the training center spent so much time reviewing what Christ did and that He died for us, showed us what was important. This ends up being the central thing that we learned. Everything was built upon that. I understood that if I came to know the Gospel, then I would be able to share it more effectively using any method that I could find.

# Practical Aspects of Ministry

- I learned how to interact with people, and I know how to deal with people now. The training center taught me how to take any theme, on any religion, any theme about Christianity, and how to steer it to the essence of the Gospel, the mercy of God, grace, and forgiveness.
- The training center aided me in knowing how to talk with people. Although I thought I knew what it meant to talk with people and how to approach them with the Gospel, many times I made mistakes and the results hurt the ministry more than helped it. What I received in the training center allowed me to think through the process of communication and work on improving my interpersonal skills.

- Probably most important for me was that I learned how to approach people, value people, see people as people, and then share the Gospel with them.

# God's Call

When asked "Why do you continue to serve?" or "What motivates you in ministry?" many church planters responded that God had called them to minister. Some of them focused on the sense of satisfaction they felt doing God's will, saying that ministry gives purpose or meaning in life.

- Those who are called, and God has called me, cannot live without serving Him. I have to share. My old self is dead and buried and now I'm living in Christ.
- God has called me to this. I didn't seek it.
- I know I don't have the qualities needed, the skills needed, but I realize that God has called me and gives me all that I need to do His will.
- The call of God is like my bread, the essence of who I am. It is bread for my soul.
- Honestly, I can't even imagine life without ministry; it would be an empty life. I serve because it is my life. I can't imagine doing anything different.
- I have great joy to be with these people, to see what the Lord is doing. It is a great privilege to be with Him and serve Him. I love these people.
- I can't live any differently. What God has done in my life is so dramatic, I have changed and I can't go back to what it was before.

Just as He did during New Testament times, God still uses imperfect people to accomplish His purposes. This applies to all cultures and time periods. He waits for those who will recognize His call and say, "Here am I; send me."

# 10

# Who are the Least of These and How Do We Serve Them?

by Pamela L. Sanders

In September of 2000, our group began ministering to Mexico City college students in a brand-new campus ministry, El Oasis. We were all recent graduates of the same university in the U.S. and had gotten to know one another through our involvement in a campus ministry there. Early on, we knew we wanted to serve the "least of these" in Mexico City. We wanted to be Jesus' hands and feet in a world in need of love and grace, living out the message of Christ and showing God's love in a real way. Our difficulty was that we did not have any idea where to begin or even who the "least of these" were in this huge city.

After making phone calls and coordinating some small-scale service projects on our own, we realized that we could be more effective if we teamed up with other service organizations that could provide expertise and ongoing opportunities.

This is a story about how we developed an amazing relationship with a ministry that works with children, teenagers, and young adults who live on the streets, Lampas International.

This partnership has made the impossible task of directly serving Mexico City street kids through El Oasis a reality.

# Overview of the Campus Ministry

El Oasis is a Christian ministry for Mexico City college students. We are modeled after campus ministries in the United States, specifically the Christian Campus Fellowship at the Georgia Institute of Technology. At El Oasis we have applied and adapted this U.S. model of college ministry to Mexico City and its specific cultural context. The goal of our ministry is to transform the lives of Mexico City college students with Jesus' love and grace. Through community and teaching we encourage spiritual growth that challenges students to follow the teachings of Jesus, experience and share his love, and change their lives through faith in him. After five years of existence, El Oasis has approximately 80 students involved in the ministry who represent more than 10 different universities.

One of the most important parts of our ministry is a weekly community gathering in which one of the team members gives a talk relating a biblical passage to the students' everyday lives. The worship team leads praise and song in addition to skits, videos and other creative activities. Through this meeting, as well as small groups and retreats, students experience community and spiritual growth. Small groups are a safe place where students study the Bible and develop deep friendships. Through fellowship the students encourage one another, share their lives with one another, and push each other to grow. Retreats are a weekend away full of activities that deepen faith and community for both consistent participants and newcomers.

A key focus of our ministry is outreach to the students on their college campuses. This is done by our staff, Mexican students who are a part of the El Oasis community, and exchange students from the U.S. who study in Mexico for a semester and assist our ministry. These exchange students make friends as they get involved on the university campuses and then invite those friends to El Oasis activities. Many of these cross-cultural friendships have effectively shown God's love and allowed Mexican students to experience this love in the El Oasis community.

Over the years we have hosted a variety of non-threatening activities like English classes, English conversation groups, basketball and soccer games, free cinnamon rolls in the grass outside the Freshman classrooms, and biscuits, cookies, coffee and tea while sitting on blankets or on the grass in the middle of campus.

# Service Projects

At El Oasis we felt called to serve some of the over 20 million inhabitants of the city. In the beginning as we searched for opportunities to involve our community in social service, we wanted to find opportunities that would be available regularly so that we could build on our experiences and relationships, but not exhaust the limited resources of our small fledgling ministry of mostly full-time college students. We decided to have one major social service project on a Saturday each month, called Sábado de Servicio (Service Saturday).

The goal of these Saturdays is to increase our college students' awareness of the difficult realities of many around them, and to demonstrate God's love by providing for and meeting the needs of the people we are serving in a practical way. It is also a great way for new students to be introduced to El Oasis and begin to get involved. More than 90% of the students who arrive at El Oasis are not involved in any church or religious community and often have strong aversions to anything associated with religion. Frequently these barriers are overcome by first participating in one of our campus outreach activities, social activities or a community social service project. As they see the joy, fun, and friendships in students, and the ways in which the ministry serves those in need around us, many students decide that the community might be worth exploring.

Our Service Saturdays include visits to nursing homes, orphanages, women's prisons, and children in the hospital. As we began to meet more people in need, as well as the organizations serving them, we gradually developed solid relationships with dedicated groups such as Lampas International.

# Street Kids

In Mexico City, over 250,000 kids live on the streets. Many come from situations of abuse or abandonment, and most use drugs to escape their realities. These children and teenagers live in metro stations, abandoned buildings, parks, or sewers, or roam from one place to another. They live in danger of other street kids and police. They beg, steal, and sometimes are involved in prostitution in order to survive. In response to this situation, in December 1990 Jesús Gutiérrez, who used to live on the streets of Argentina, formed the ministry Lampas International.

Throughout the year Lampas organizes special activities such as sports events, parties for Christmas and other special days, Bible conferences, and camps. The camps are a unique opportunity for these youth to leave the streets for a week and participate in activities outside of Mexico City. Lampas provides transportation to the camp, three meals a day, showers, clean clothes, and a plethora of fun activities including soccer, basketball, volleyball, games, movies, and a campfire. Throughout the week there are Bible lessons, as well as an opportunity at the end of the week for the kids to share their experiences of how God has been working in their lives and to dedicate their lives to God.

Many street kids have made changes in their lives, left the streets, and decided to follow Christ after these camps. Some have even decided to attend the Jireh Bible Institute, also run by Lampas. Jireh is designed for former street kids and others who want to learn more about the Bible in an intensive three year program that includes Bible training, discipling in Christian living, and practical work training in fields such as carpentry. In Lampas' fifteen years of existence, they have worked with over 12,000 street kids, almost all of whom have heard the gospel.

# Partnering with a Purpose

Our relationship with Lampas started when we asked Joy, a young woman who was working with them in ministry and had formerly lived on the streets, to come give her testimony to a group of El Oasis college women. She told us about her alcoholic step-father who would hit her and her mother, brothers, and sisters. At the age of eleven Joy left her family in Vera Cruz and five years later found herself on the streets of Mexico City. There she met others like herself who had abandoned their families and who invited Joy to be a part of their community.

In this new family of youth living on the streets, Joy was introduced to a lifestyle of drugs and mischief. Joy described her life on the streets in sometimes contradictory terms. She experienced very difficult moments that included being cold, hungry, and lonely. She described a general lack of respect in the midst of a community that took care of each other. She shared with us about the violence of the police who would come to them asking for drugs and money. Joy told us of being filled with sadness, of how she and many of her friends felt lost because they felt that their parents did not love them. Many used drugs to escape these realities, many wanted to die, and some did.

The last time I visited Kangemi slum, I nearly didn't make it out. It had rained for two solid hours during the Sunday service at Faith Victory Christian Church, a small church in the Nairobi River valley. When I left, the little track was so steep and slick that it took several runs up the rutted hillside and a crowd to push. I nearly wiped out a series of temporary shops and houses thrown up along the narrow path.

Six people from Faith Victory had trained with us in Community Health Evangelism (CHE), so our team had returned to observe the seed project that the church and community were attempting. We weren't sure what to expect. In CHE terminology, a seed project is a project used in the early stages of mobilizing communities to become what God wants them to be. This simple project is to raise awareness, create visibility, build enthusiasm, and help the church show God's love to the community in a practical way.

The training team from Faith Victory along with the community had determined that a footbridge was needed across a deep ravine that divided the community. The current bridge consisted of one log: dangerous for one adult with no load when it was dry; treacherous for women with babies on their backs or heavy loads; horrendous for school children when it rained and turned the trickle of water below to a raging torrent. When it rained, the log became as slick as ice. Children had drowned because they didn't like the alternative of a two- or three-kilometer detour around the ravine. A number of adults had broken bones falling off the log.

Faith Victory's Pastor Augustine had done an excellent job of preparation. His church prayed and fasted every Tuesday for their community. He approached the government officials and received their blessing. He involved some landlords after they got over an initial fear of a tenant revolt against poor living conditions. The poor people in the slum collected enough money to get wood, poles, and nails to build with.

What would we find when we showed up: few church folks, materials lacking, no expertise to complete the task? Work would start at 9 a.m., but thinking that nothing would happen by then, we arrived a little after 11. What we found was  astounding. The bridge was nearly complete! A local landlord was leading in the digging, sawing, and pounding of nails. Over 40 men from the community were helping. At least one hundred children were running around excited. Others watched with keen interest as they went about their business. Women marveled as they began to use the bridge.

Later, over a meal prepared by the church ladies, the community made plans to form a committee. They already had a list of tasks they want to complete. For many, it was their first time in the church building. Yet all were caught up in the church's enthusiasm, celebrating how God had helped them do a great thing. God was glorified!

What had happened with the Kangemi slum seed project that stirred up so much interest, and enthusiasm, and set off a flurry of activity? Certainly the bridge will win no worldly awards for beauty and architectural design. The local people's lives did not experience the type of economic change that will qualify them to be featured on "Lifestyles of the Rich and Famous." Hundreds did not receive salvation. But something had occurred that has made a difference in individual lives and in the community as a whole.

Some time later, I went back to ask Pastor Augustine for insight. Still very excited, he described how people had come together. The rich and powerful worked with the extremely poor and powerless. Walls of suspicion between tribes came down as they worked together instead of just for their own group. A number of Christians from different churches were involved. Many responded with surprise when they found out who the other Christians were in their community. The non-Christians and Christians worked together in community. "Before, we were afraid of each other," said Pastor Augustine. All kinds of people came together, praised God, and prayed for success. Relationships were restored. God and man were in touch, even if briefly.

Some experts feel that poverty begins because of bad and broken relationships. When relationships are restored through the power of the Holy Spirit, then communities can come together and improve their spiritual and physical lives. The bridge, while extremely practical, is also a symbol of restored relationships.

One night a taxi trying to escape the police for having an unroadworthy vehicle flew down the hill and came to the bridge. His car could not get back up the hill, so he wanted to drive over the footbridge. Folks from every part of the community came running out in the night to protect their bridge. Eventually they let him pass, but only after he signed a note saying he would pay for any damages.

As Pastor Augustine leads this group, he now says with confidence,. "I am no longer afraid to approach anyone. God is with this community."

**Garry, serving in Kenya**

Joy lived on the streets for three years before she began talking to people from Lampas about God and eternal life. Joy was tired of her life and in her emptiness wondered if there really was a God that loved her and could change her life. Eventually Joy decided to leave the streets; she moved in with two Lampas workers and began to study the Bible. Her desire to serve became stronger and she studied at a Bible Institute for three years before joining Lampas in their work.

Her story opened many of our students' eyes to another world that they knew nothing about in areas not far from their own homes. Joy's story of the realities she had to face as a street kid, how she met Jesus, left the streets, and later worked ministering to the same communities she had left, produced in our community a profound desire to help. We contacted Lampas and soon after held our first Service Saturday serving street kids. Our project leader that day was Joy. After that we were able to do an average of one outreach per semester working with Lampas.

This partnership has been beneficial to both ministries. Lampas provides the expertise, knowledge, and experience required to be able to find the street kids, establish trusting relationships, and train our students in appropriate interaction with this population. They also offer us guidance on how to deal with difficult situations.

El Oasis is able to provide important resources of food, drink, clothing, and games, in addition to many young people who desire to serve. We are able to have both meaningful and trivial conversations, expressing trust and friendship in simple ways. Our students' and staffs' lives have been changed from these experiences. We became humbled as we saw smiles on the street kids' faces with such little effort on our part. All we had to do was show up, play, laugh, talk, and love to make one or two of these kids feel more loved and accepted.

# "Let's Do a Camp Together"

After several years of various Saturday events, we decided that we would like to partner with Lampas to do a week-long camp. El Oasis was able to obtain funding for the week and provide enough students to make the logistics of the camp possible. We started the week by dividing our volunteers into small groups to go to the different locations where the street kids lived to make sure they were awake and then take them on the metro to the bus waiting to transport them. It was early in the morning and many of the street kids were still on drugs from the night before. As we accompanied them on the metro, the other people riding would move away from us and stare. From the very beginning of the first day our students began to see what life was like for street kids.

As all of the groups arrived, the kids were checked for drugs before being permitted to get on the bus. Upon arrival at the camp the first activity was bathing in the showers, which left quite a stench. Amazingly the odor and the dirt were still very present on most of the children even after they emerged from their showers. The showers were connected to the sleeping areas and our students slept in the same rooms as the street kids. These close living quarters made for some uncomfortable moments, especially early in the week. Eating together was shocking at first as the street kids put their hands all over the food as they eagerly grabbed for tortillas, beans, and whatever was being served. They threw back on the table what they did not want. Taking food after it had been handled by so many unwashed hands was difficult for many from our group.

For the week, everyone was divided into two teams, which competed against each other in a variety of games, contests, and sports. Besides these competitions, each day there was a Bible teaching time, meals and a movie. The El Oasis students and staff were responsible for participating in all the events, serving the food at each meal, washing dishes, cleaning the bathrooms, and whatever else we were asked to do. Each day was completely full and the students and the street kids gave their all.

Tyson, the nickname of one of the street youth, was a natural leader. His vibrant personality attracted others. He was excited to be at this camp and his enthusiasm helped make the week a positive experience for many. The others respected Tyson and what he said definitely mattered. At the end of the week Tyson decided to stay at the camp, where the Jireh Bible Institute was located, for more time so that he could learn more and attempt living in a different way, off the streets.

One of the children, Toño, became very close with Angel, one of our students. Toño was one of the few who did not use drugs. During some long conversations, Angel encouraged Toño to remain firm and to not fall into a drug addiction. After the camp, several of our students continued to visit Toño at his metro stop, often getting coffee or lunch together.

All of this hard work at the camp allowed Lampas to deepen their relationships with the street kids as well as share the gospel with them on various occasions. For our students this experience served to remove many of their prejudices and pre-conceived ideas about street kids as they lived together in close quarters and began to understand each other more.

Our students also learned to serve on a much deeper level than they had ever experienced. El Oasis participants did what the Lampas staff needed, which did not always mean serving in the ways they felt gifted in or comfortable with—cleaning bathrooms, playing sports or helping with other tasks without complaining. They learned that serving is not always fun and that certain things must get done in order to achieve the goals and meet the real needs of the kids. This shared experience not only taught us more about service, but it also united us as a team and as friends. It was a difficult yet rewarding week in which our community learned much as the street kids experienced God's love and heard God's message of grace.

# Advancing the Kingdom

El Oasis and Lampas both strive to share God's love and grace in the world around us. The manifestations of our ministries and certainly the needs of our focus populations are often very different. However, through partnership we found that our organizations could work together to achieve common goals.

We at El Oasis are honored to be able to participate in ministry with the street kids of Mexico City. We often wonder if it is the street kids or the college students who receive more from this interaction as both groups learn about love, grace, humility, suffering, and joy. Regardless, we are convinced that everyone involved walks away from each experience with a glimpse of God's love for all people and a better understanding of how God wants us to manifest that love in the world in which we live. We hope that our partnership with Lampas, as well as our partnerships with other service organizations, continues to grow into new and exciting endeavors that advance the kingdom of God here on earth.

At the beginning of our Community Health and Evangelism (CHE—a Christian community development program) training program, considerable time is devoted to understanding the meaning of development: development in relation to community, development as opposed to relief, community development under the Lordship of Jesus Christ. The goal of a successful CHE program is equipping, enabling, and involving the people in how to problem-solve the needs they have recognized in their community. When this strategy is placed under God's direction, a transformed community is developed as people experience the abundant life Christ desires for His family.

This is a skit called "The River Crossing" that introduces the concept of development. Two lines are drawn with chalk on the floor, representing the banks of a river. A large circle is drawn in the middle of the river to represent an island. Four smaller circles are drawn representing stepping stones, two on each side of the island.

Then the action begins. Two men come to the river and want to cross but do not know how to swim. The current is strong, and they are afraid to cross. A third man comes along and sees their difficulty. He offers to help them cross on the stepping stones, but they are afraid. He agrees to carry one on his back, but only manages to reach the island, where he leaves the first man. He then returns to the riverbank to get the second man. But because he is now too tired, he refuses to carry the man. Instead, he agrees to help him walk across on the stones. Halfway across, the second man feels confident enough to manage on his own. Both men cross the river while the first man is left on the island. He shouts for help as the two walk away, forgetting that he has been left behind.

We stop the action at this point and ask the onlooking audience (people of the community) what took place. The message that comes from this skit, of course, is that when you do something for someone it does not teach them how to do it themselves. That is a relief. Facilitated discussion ensues regarding the key points to glean from this skit and how to apply them to the community.

The lessons learned from this story
form the crux of CHE:

- Doing something for someone does not teach him/her how to do it.
- There is more motivation to learn when there is a need.
- We learn by example.
- Using local resources whenever possible is wise.
- And, finally, that when the developer leaves and the people have not been taught, the project dies.

As the skit resumes, the man that was helped across the river goes back to the man who was left on the island and teaches him how to cross.

**Judy, serving in Ivory Coast**

# 11

# Sharing the Gospel on Treadmills and Spin Bikes

by Janet Smith

John and James are missionaries in a large, bustling city in Asia. When they begin their day, however, they don't go to a church building, a medical clinic, or a school. They go to a first-class fitness facility frequented daily by hundreds of upper-middle-class nationals. None of them know that John and James are marketplace ministers, but all of them know they are Christians.

The Fitness & Learning Center is an innovative approach to sharing the gospel using the business as mission model, a first-century idea taking on new life as an important method of doing missions in the 21st century. This approach is often used in "creative access countries" where traditional missionaries cannot get residential visas.

In 2000 a two-year research project was begun to determine a business platform that would attract middle-class nationals to a venue where they could interact regularly with resident missionaries. Asians have a growing interest in fitness. So an American-style fitness center was selected as the pilot business-as-mission project in the country.

The team leader and his staff looked at several locations where the center would be visible and accessible to its target market. Several church partners provided initial funds to help totally renovate the selected building. All of the construction work was monitored by two volunteer American engineers. A business plan was developed under the oversight of a retired Indianapolis business owner. The team's goal was a first-class, well run facility appealing to the nearby students, business people, and families.

The center opened in January 2006. Currently, there are about 700 members and 15 national employees. Rather than using stethoscopes, classrooms, or preaching services to reach out to seekers, John and James and their families use exercise classes, bike marathons, and a juice bar to build relationships and community among the members and employees of their fitness center. All the while, they teach and model spiritual values and a Christ-centered lifestyle.

The team uses a variety of ministry activities to reach out to the members and the community. Last Christmas, gym members adopted 47 children who live in a local AIDS orphanage, purchasing clothes and toys for these poorest of the poor. They have also provided clothing for displaced political refugees.

An American Christian personal trainer, working at the facility on a short-term basis, brought together a large group to train for a triathlon, which brought an increased sense of community to the membership. James and John also spend a great deal of time counseling members who come to them for help with personal and spiritual problems.

The nationals on staff at the gym are a primary focus of mission activity. John and James and their families held a Christmas party for them where they shared the gospel story. Some of the gym's Christian members pray regularly for the staff, witness to them, and have taken some of them to church. A local church has agreed to teach character-building seminars to the staff.

Some employees have already expressed surprise that the center honors the country's complicated business structure by paying all the required taxes, which is not a common business practice there. However, these are people who had no exposure to Christianity before coming to the gym, and now they have repeated exposure to Christian values, the love of Christ, and the gospel message. John acknowledges that it is a slow process to move them forward.

Very soon, John and James plan to put a cross on the gym wall. "The staff wanted us to put up a 'spirit house' to help sell memberships," said John, "so we decided to put up the cross as a symbol of a living Spirit, and a testimony that our business is run by devoted Christians." In the future, they plan to use the gym as a focal point for a church plant for middle-class nationals.

John, the general manager, is quick to point out that the fitness center is not a "front" for mission work, or simply a platform for entry visas. "This is real business, real stuff, and we have to work hard to stay afloat, just like any other business," he said.

The business provides John and James with the credentials they need to live and work in the country, as well as credibility with their friends and employees. It also gives them access for ministry to many others who come into contact with the business, such as vendors, other business owners in the area, and members' families. Most importantly, it offers the opportunity to build close relationships with the nationals who come to them every day, to fellowship in a church without a steeple.

Orphans, vulnerable children, AIDS babies, millions living in poverty. The situation is desperate in Nairobi, Kenya, where up to 70% of the city's 5 million people live in slums. One in every three people living in the slums carries the AIDS virus. Can anything be done?

The Christian Church of Thousand Oaks (CCTO) in California decided it must do something for the urban poor of Nairobi, particularly those devastated by HIV/AIDS. In the Mathare Valley slum, some 800,000 people live in small shanties along the hillside. There are no amenities or paved roads, only a few communal water spigots, and practically no toilets.

CCTO raised $200,000 to help the people of Kenya. Some of that money was designated for business as mission, funds specifically for microenterprise to help individuals in the slums begin small businesses.

Their contacts in Mathare Valley were Wallace and Mary Kamau, founders of Missions of Hope. The Kamaus were introduced to CCTO by resident missionaries Keith and Kathy Ham, who have worked in Mathare Valley for seven years, beginning their ministry by establishing a school for the poorest children. When the school opened, community leaders were asked to identify the neediest people in the community. Students were enrolled from this list of children. As children come to interview for a place in the school, Mary and her team visit each child's shanty to learn more about his or her background—a fertile strategy for evangelism.

One mother, Elizabeth, was able to secure a place for her child. Elizabeth was a heavy drinker. Her job was collecting firewood from the forest, a difficult job because men guarding the forest required bribes to enter it, which Elizabeth and other women like her could not afford. They were forced to pay with their bodies.

During an open-air meeting in Mathare, Elizabeth came forward and committed her life to Christ. This was difficult because it meant a lifestyle change and she literally could not walk since she had been drinking. Mary knew follow-up would be vital to keep the young woman focused on her decision, so she went to Elizabeth's shanty before

she left for the forest the next morning. Elizabeth said she could not remember making a commitment and could not be born again anyway because of her job. Mary reminded her that whether she remembered the commitment or not, God did—then counseled and prayed with her.

At the end of the prayer, Elizabeth said she would have to do something different to make money. Mary asked, "If you had money to start a business, what would you like to do?" Elizabeth said she knew how to make chapatis (flat bread), and could sell those. Mary loaned her $8 to buy the supplies. That very day Elizabeth began her business, which now provides an adequate income for her and her two daughters. A new perspective and a small loan totally changed her life.

Today Elizabeth knows God as provider. He provided a way for her to change the direction of her life by providing people who met her spiritual and physical needs. She has joined a church, become a baptized believer, and is actively involved in the church's choir ministry. Elizabeth represents microenterprise and business as mission at its finest.

**Caleb, preparing for service**

# 12
# Building the Kingdom Brick by Brick

by Lyndon and Denise Pesho*

We never envisioned ourselves as brick makers or brick merchants. We are trained and have served for more than thirty years as evangelists and teachers of the Word. In general we have been more at home in the sanctuary than in the marketplace.

When we came to this populous Southeast Asian nation we had official documents that identified us as missionaries. We even filed work plans with the government defining our efforts to assist the government's program of moral education by teaching the Bible, gathering groups and eventually forming them into churches. For more than 15 years after the failed communist coup of the mid-1960s this was an acceptable role in the areas where communism had been strong and the place of Islam generally superficial.

As the influence of Islam, financed by increased wealth from oil in the Muslim Middle East, grew throughout the land, missionary evangelists began to experience more and more pressure. Some were forced to leave, having their resident permits revoked. All who remained were required to be involved

* *not their real names*

in formal training programs, showing how they were training local people to take over their role, which in and of itself is a very biblical concept and good missiology. Unfortunately, once the training was complete the foreign worker was expected to leave, not to move on to another location and start the program over again.

After we became involved in a formal training program, equipping local evangelists, students who came to study with us broadened our vision from the island where we had lived, showing us vast unreached areas of the nation. We soon developed a burden to see the gospel penetrate these by-passed peoples. Most of these people have an intense identity with Islam. The strategies of the past will not work among them.

As the Lord began to gather a ministry team for a cluster of peoples we will refer to as the Johor, we grappled with how to identify ourselves so that we might be able to live among them, building friendships strong enough to allow the message of the gospel to be accurately and lovingly communicated. We found our target people to be rather suspicious. We did not look like the typical back-packing hippies who come to teach English – something we tried. We tried a few small business efforts for the local workers who joined us in the effort – none proved viable. Perhaps we were overly concerned with looking like we were doing business rather than really doing business!

After we had struggled with this concept for almost three years, we still had nothing solid enough to get our people out of the major city of Johor-land. This was especially important because we increasingly felt the need to focus on a small branch who were primarily rural.

A congregation in Singapore had been introduced to the Johor people by a former co-worker who was a member there serving as a Regional Director for an agency based in Indiana. He had played a significant role in helping us identify the Johor cluster of peoples as our target. This fellowship formally and seriously "adopted" the rural Johor as their people group, committing themselves to do whatever it takes for as long as is required to see a reproducing church planting movement among the Johor people. Ho Kwai is a member of the congregation who has taken this adoption commitment to heart.

In 2002 Ho Kwai was in the right place at the right time to overhear plans for the development of a new industry in Singapore. At a transition point professionally, he pursued this opportunity with diligence. He established a partnership with a German company that is the world leader in this industry and began to position himself for the opening of the market in Singapore. Early in the process he realized that it might be something that could bless his "adopted" people group as well.

The industry requires a large quantity of crushed clay chips. Among the rural Johor there are many traditional brick makers and enough workers to manually process them to the required size for use in his industry. Urged on by Ho Kwai, several in our team began the process of learning about making good bricks, how to set up and operate a business in this land, etc. All the time we were learning about business the Lord was teaching us patience and reliance. The Singapore market began to develop in 2006.

Our plan is simple: team members act as purchasing agents and quality control staff. They choose the bricks, have them crushed, checking the standard of the sieving, and then warehouse and ship them to our customer in Singapore where they are used in the developing market there. It now looks promising to have a regular stream of shipments leaving Johor-land for Singapore.

The purchasing agents, quality control staff and crushing supervisors are all team members with a heart for the eternal salvation of all involved in the process. With this business we are welcome; our identities are no longer suspect. Relationships are developing.

Salim was the first rural Johor man to walk the mud brick road into the Kingdom. He was a brickmaker at the team operated site. Abdul shared with him, developed a deepening relationship, and eventually helped him take a cleansing bath in the river. He now seeks to reach out to others in his community and family. We are trusting that as more roads of mud brick are built into Johor villages, many "beautiful feet" will walk these paths, bringing the good news, bringing rural Johor friends along those paths to our Savior.

The brick project in Johor-land has seen several kingdom forces blend together harmoniously. We come from a small group based in Georgia; the couple who guides the day-to-day production process came to us from an agency based in the midwest after many years of fruitful work in both East and West Africa. The role of the Indiana-based agency mentioned above has been very significant. The ministry was envisioned and is guided commercially by the businessmen of the congregation in Singapore. Singaporean believers together with a congregation in Colorado have given significant start-up capital. We have been blessed to see so many "organs" of the body work together efficiently and respectfully with virtually no tension.

While this project was developing, albeit more slowly than we had dreamed, we were privileged to be involved in a spin-off project which is blessing another strong Muslim people group from the part of our country which was hit by a mammoth tsunami in late 2004.

Again, the Lord brought together a unique team. As we sought a way to bless the people of the province where 170,000 people died early one morning, an Indiana-based relief agency expressed a willingness to provide funds to assist. This assistance allowed an avenue for kingdom workers to enter this area with help and love to assist these hurting people with all of their needs, immediate and eternal.

First a plan had to be formulated and a work area identified. The Lord brought three wonderful couples together again. We had been privileged to work alongside all three of these couples 25 years earlier. The Lord led them to a neglected and needy area where little was being done by the larger relief agencies.

Many homes had been destroyed in a nearby town. The temporary tents were quickly deteriorating. Many forms of employment had been washed away by the waves. A cash-for-work project to help with tsunami-related clean-up and to get income into the community was developed. This was followed by a housing program to get families out of tents and into small, simple wooden houses. A longer term employment-generating operation was also put into place. Seeing the mammoth construction needs in rebuilding schools, offices, and shops, it was that apparent there would be a need for a virtually endless supply of brick. Prior to the team's arrival, the closest brick- makers in operation were 3 or 4 hours away over barely passable roads.

Members of the Johor team were able to give a crash course in brick-making to a quickly recruited team who would try to use the basic philosophies of building pathways for the gospel with local mud bricks. These evangelists-cum-entrepreneurs were assisted by Jabril, the person in charge of the rural Johor brick business in laying out a brick-making site and getting into production.

Their bricks are being praised for their quality, often resulting in competing offers from contractors to buy them as fast as they come out of the firing. The Indiana-based relief agency provided the set-up capital in a location that had been identified by members of a research team. The team added other gospel workers partnering in making bricks, bricks to build the Kingdom.

By God's grace, as many partner together in unity, brick can be used to build the kingdom of God.

# Contributors

*Carol Plymale* and her husband Virgil are retired full-time RV'ers who travel and spend part of each year volunteering for different organizations.

*Janice Lemke* serves in Ukraine and is the author of *Five Loaves and Two Bowls of Borscht*.

*Luis Bush* is the international facilitator for Transform World Connections.

*Ashley Barker* lives with the urban poor in Bangkok, Thailand and is the founder of Urban Neighbors of Hope.

*Bryant L. Myers* is Professor of Transformational Development at the School of Intercultural Studies of Fuller Theological Seminary.

*Charles Van Engen* is Professor of Biblical Theology of Mission at the School of Intercultural Studies of Fuller Theological Seminary.

*Doug Priest* is the Executive Director of Christian Missionary Fellowship.

*Florence Muindi* is the founder of Life in Abundance, a mission agency serving in many African countries.

*Cory and Janice Lemke* are with CMF International in Ukraine and helped found the Efas Training Center in Crimea.

*Pamela L. Sanders* served in Mexico City as part of a Globalscope campus ministry team.

*Janet Smith* serves with the Marketplace Ministries Division of CMF International.

*Lyndon and Denise Pesho* are pseudonyms used by a Christian couple residing in Southeast Asia.

# Acknowledgements

Chapter Three appeared in *Missiology*, 2005. 33:1:17-28. Adapted and used by permission.

Chapter Four contains excerpts from the book *Make Poverty Personal: The Bible's Call to End Oppression,* by Ash Barker. Published in 2006 by Urban Neighbours of Hope. Springvale, Australia. Used by permission.

Chapter Five appeared in *The Brandywine Review of Faith & International Affairs*, 2004. 2:3:51-55. Used by permission.

Chapter Six appeared in the on-line journal *Global Missiology*, October 2005. www.globalmissiology.org. Adapted and used by permission.

Chapter Seven is taken from the book *The Hope Factor: Engaging the Church in the HIV/AIDS Crisis*, edited by Tetsuanao Yamamori, David Dageforde and Tina Bruner. Published in 2003 by Authentic Media. Waynesboro, Georgia. 303-306. Used by permission.

Chapter Eight was presented at a conference entitled "Health and Wholeness for the 21st Century," Chiang Mai, Thailand, Oct. 17-22, 2003. Used by permission.

Chapter Eleven appeared in *Christian Standard*, Aug. 19, 2007. 6-7. Used by permission.

Pages 4, 22 and 23 appeared in a brochure entitled "Many Stories, One Author," published in 2003 by Christian Missionary Fellowship.

Pages 30, 31, 72 and 111 appeared in *Impact*, 2002, 52:1. Published by Christian Missionary Fellowship.

Pages 34-36 appeared in *The Southeast Outlook*, published by Southeast Christian Church. Dec. 22 and Dec. 29, 2005. Used by permission.

Pages 43, 67, 80-81, and 97 are taken from the book *Surrender All: A Call to Submerge with Christ* by Ashley Barker. Published in 2005 by Urban Neighbours of Hope. Springvale, Australia. Used by permission.

Pages 53-55 appeared in a prayer newsletter published in July 2005 by CMF International.

Pages 63-65 are taken from the book *Make Poverty Personal* by Ash Barker. Published in 2006 by Urban Neighbours of Hope. Springvale, Australia. Used by permission.

Pages 101-102 appeared in *Christian Standard*, May 30, 2004. 7. Used by permission.

Pages 106-108 are adapted from 1st Caribbean HIV and Development Workshop, Facilitators Manual, United Nations Development Program.

Pages 130-132 appeared in *Impact*, 2005, 54:1. Published by Christian Missionary Fellowship.

Pages 137-138 appeared in a prayer newsletter published in March 2006 by CMF.

Pages 142-143 appeared in *Christian Standard*, Aug. 19, 2007. 5. Used by permission.